, like, . . . . . . . . . .
. . . . . . . , like, . .
. . , like, . . . . . . .
ike, . . . . . . . . . .
. . . . . . . , **like**, .
like, . . . . . . . . .
. . . . , like, . . . . .
. . . . . . . . , like,
, like, . . . . . . . . .
. . . . . . . , like, . .
. . , like, . . . . . .

# Like

## A History of the World's Most Hated (and Misunderstood) Word

**Megan C. Reynolds**

HarperOne
*An Imprint of HarperCollinsPublishers*

Without limiting the exclusive rights of any author, contributor or the publisher of this publication, any unauthorized use of this publication to train generative artificial intelligence (AI) technologies is expressly prohibited. HarperCollins also exercise their rights under Article 4(3) of the Digital Single Market Directive 2019/790 and expressly reserve this publication from the text and data mining exception.

LIKE. Copyright © 2025 by Megan C. Reynolds. All rights reserved. Printed in the United States of America. No part of this book may be used or reproduced in any manner whatsoever without written permission except in the case of brief quotations embodied in critical articles and reviews. For information, address HarperCollins Publishers, 195 Broadway, New York, NY 10007. In Europe, HarperCollins Publishers, Macken House, 39/40 Mayor Street Upper, Dublin 1, D01 C9W8, Ireland.

HarperCollins books may be purchased for educational, business, or sales promotional use. For information, please email the Special Markets Department at SPsales@harpercollins.com.

harpercollins.com

FIRST EDITION

*Designed by Yvonne Chan*

Library of Congress Cataloging-in-Publication Data has been applied for.

ISBN 978-0-06-341528-7

25 26 27 28 29 LBC 5 4 3 2 1

For my mother who gave me her face and her charm,
and for my father who let me read whatever I wanted.

# Contents

**Introduction: Like, Why?** 1

**Chapter 1: Like, What?** 19

Interlude: The Grammar Wars 40

**Chapter 2: And *Then* I Was Like . . .** 47

**Chapter 3: Well, Like, I Just, I'm Not, Like, Sure . . .** 63

Interlude: But What About Texting? 88

Interlude: Brass Tacks (Dictionaries) 92

**Chapter 4: I Have, Like, One Zillion Things to Do** 97

Interlude: Why Is It Women? 115

**Chapter 5: Like, It's Sexist?** 121

Interlude: Girls on Film 140

Interlude: How Do People Learn English? 154

Interlude: Nǐ Shuō Shénme?! 159

**Chapter 6: That's, Like, Not Very Professional** 169

**Chapter 7: Like . . . !** 195

**Conclusion: Like, What's Next?** 213

References 233

Acknowledgments 243

**Introduction**

# Like, Why?

I have always been someone who strives to be careful with my words, because I am of the firm belief that what I say and, more importantly, *how* I say it matters. Brevity is not my forte; personally, the only way to get my point across is to use as many of the *right* words as possible, each one carefully selected for maximum impact. Surely this has something to do with my unyielding desire to know the outcome of any situation at any given time—the slightly anxious person's yen for control over the uncontrollable. My logic is as follows: If I say the right thing at the right time, my intentions will be clear. If I am careful with my words, my meaning will never be misconstrued. I'm proving a point, but I'm also proving myself. Avoiding the affliction of misspeaking—once rudely referred to as "verbal diarrhea" by a cousin to whom I no longer speak—has served me well enough in my adult life. Though I maintain that my loquacious nature is nothing more than a charming personality quirk, enough time (and therapy) has proven otherwise. Sometimes the best way to face yourself and to get your point across is, after all, the simplest one.

Mastering a vocabulary full of "ten-dollar words," as my mother calls them, is a crutch—it's much harder to say what you feel rather than what you mean, as the latter is all context and the former, the point. Understanding this has been instrumental in figuring out how to communicate with other people and has allowed me to be hyperaware of how I speak and what I'm actually saying. This is a skill set that most people have even if they don't actually use it; unfortunately for women, it's a skill set that has evolved out of necessity. I am a helper in many aspects of my life; part of this particular sickness is accommodation, but especially in conversations or situations that don't necessarily warrant it. I don't love conflict, and sometimes it's just nice to take the easy way out—to set aside my feelings and modulate my response in part so that the other person (and, in turn, myself) is more comfortable.

I'm careful with my speech, so much so that I speak in circles. "Get to the point," my therapist will say to me as I unfurl a monologue that explains *why* I feel the way I do and what I think I should do about it, neatly sidestepping the heart of the actual matter, which is my feelings. Unlearning my verbal tendency to overexplain, to intellectualize the emotional, and to predict the outcome of a conversation that could be uncomfortable or otherwise upsetting are lifelong tasks. But when I take the time to sit down and really look at what I'm saying and how I say it, I've noticed that the word I use, time and time again, when there are seemingly so many others at my grasp, is "like."

Let us not beat around the bush: Everybody says "like,"

whether they like it or not. The word is likely a habitual part of your regular, everyday speech. If you really start to pick apart your own speech patterns, you will find yourself overwhelmed with and pleasantly surprised at how often "like" works its way in. Blessedly, the only times I am treated to the sound of my own voice as a listener is when I play back interview recordings or the voice notes I send to my friends when I don't feel like typing. But "like" shows up in a lot of places, even in the sort of written communication that *feels* like speaking, like the backlogs of my text messages or, worse, a Slack channel that I share with friends who are former coworkers. It gets in where it fits in, in the places where grammar prescriptivists and cranky op-ed writers don't think it needs to be.

Some examples of things I haven't said but would say, as I am clearly saying them now:

> I need a side table that, like, approximates the energy of a late-seventies key party—so, like, nasty but chic, like a table that someone may or may not use for cocaine, but honestly, like, probably not?

> My mother was like, "I'm gonna run a marathon," and I was like, "... Okay, girl! Best of luck!"

> I'm, like, ninety-eight years old now, so I can no longer stay out past ten.

> Like ... Okay?

# Like

I, like . . . I don't know, like, I'm not actually upset, but, like, ambiently upset?

At first blush, this is alarming. I'm a smart enough person who used to spend precious daylight hours reading books instead of climbing trees or whatever, so why do I insist on filling my speech with a word that means nothing when there are hundreds of others at my disposal? Should I change the way I communicate to sound more professional, or more "adult," or, at the very least, not like a dummy? What does it say about me as a person—and then, by extension, the rest of the world at large—if I say "like," like, *all* the time, and what, if anything at all, needs to be done to stop it?

Both these questions are rhetorical, even though I spend about four minutes a week, in total, thinking about changing the way I communicate. That is, before immediately remembering that I actually don't care that much in the first place. Yes, it's a shame that I'll never get back that time ruminating this particular quandary, but, like, whatever, it's fine, that's life.

(I'm hardly one to ring the feminist alarm bell when it's not needed, but this brief peek behind the curtain and into the brain of a woman [me] proves an annoying but pertinent point: Women's speech is always under fire, be it from the general public or, at times, from ourselves.)

The way women speak and why it is wrong is a tired old talking point trotted out by tongue-wagging pundits, and it likely will be in some capacity or another for the rest of humanity's existence. (When the fires finally come for us, it will be a blessed relief to be free of that particular line of discourse.) But then there is this unavoidable truth: Seemingly no word in the English language has come under as much fire as "like."

For all of feminism's various victories, the policing of the way women speak—which, in turn, makes women feel as if they need to police themselves, often subconsciously—is a sport that will never get old. The discourse that surrounds "like" is as sexist as the day is long, and frankly, it can be exhausting in its repetition of certain stereotypes. But there is a kernel of truth in every stereotype—women and men, for the most part, speak differently. Women are facilitators, mediators, using words carefully to ensure that conversation flows, allowing for an open dialogue. They will let someone else speak, and they will wait their turn. Men will take any opportunity they can to hold court as needed and would rather barrel through a conversation, leading the charge. "Mansplaining," a term that by now feels quaint and of a time, exists for a reason. It is a phenomenon that is rooted in truth and the universal experience of being trapped in a conversation with a man talking about NFTs.

For all the jaw-flapping men seem to do about what women are up to and why it's generally bad, it is worth noting that, by and large, women are the innovators when it comes to the evolution of language. In *Wordslut: A Feminist Guide to Taking Back the English Language*, Amanda Montell writes, "For decades, linguists have agreed that young, urban females tend to be our linguistic innovators." If, for some reason, this fact blows your mind and you're in search of a real-life example, let's take a brief journey into the heart of influencer culture—an altogether overwhelming space populated by an entire generation speaking in a bizarre patois that's a disaffected mix of marketing jargon and slang ripped from Black women and the queer community. Many influencers are women, and the way they speak is specific to their industry; there's a cadence that is particular to their craft, one that's transactional but familiar. Much like with pornography, you know it when you hear it: drawn-out pauses between words, a drawl that says, "I don't care about much, but I do want you to think I care about you."

Just like with the realization that the FedEx logo contains an arrow (FYI: It's between the second $E$ and the $x$), once you've cottoned on to the way influencers speak, you won't be able to unhear it. TikTok user and marketing major Natalya Toryanski went viral for her terrifically accurate videos skewering the "influencer cadence" adopted mostly by thin white women with a ring light and a dream. Various influencers took offense at Toryanski, herself an influencer, and then it was off to the races.

Thanks to the *Daily Mail*'s exhaustive coverage of this internecine TikTok beef, we have the details of what happened, who's mad, and why. Though Toryanski didn't call out any specific influencers, the general consensus, forged in the fire of the comments, was that she may have been referring to Emma Pritchard, an influencer with a Hailey Bieber–adjacent vibe, whose cadence and affect feel a little bit like a spot-on imitation of Toryanski's satire. Pritchard speaks as if she's bored but also interested—mostly in herself, but then, really, also in you, the viewer. There are pregnant pauses for no discernible reason; Pritchard rarely connects with the camera, but the overall effect is still alluring. I am compelled to watch "3 min GRWM | PRODUCTS I USED LINKED IN MY BIO UNDER MAKEUP FAVS" to its very end; I do not hold the left side of the screen to speed up the playback. The TikTok is casual, with a thrown-together quality, and takes place entirely in her car, as if the impulse to share compelled her to pull over and put on makeup in front of her phone for three minutes. I assume the intention of this work's casual nature is to convey relatability; you, too, could be just like Pritchard, or, more importantly, Pritchard is likable enough for you to want to stay in her orbit.

Toryanski's impersonation was spot-on because she understood what Pritchard was really doing: using the way she spoke to convey relatability and to earn trust. And yet Toryanski was criticized for this acknowledgment. The side beef that accompanied this was the women-shouldn't-make-fun-of-other-women speech, because the impersonation was supposedly tearing women down, especially those who were trying to make an honest living. According to Audra, a TikToker who went viral for her response to this kerfuffle: "Now that women, who were largely blocked out of the dignified labor market, have managed to create an industry for themselves where they can make a decent living, we're gonna pathologize their speech?"

Toryanski's response: "To say that a woman is completely exempt from criticism, to say that a woman should not be subject to criticism by another woman simply because we are of the same gender is insane, and I don't agree with that at all."

That this brief conflict was even covered gives some credence to the fact that what women say and *how* they say it seems more policed than what men say. It also gives credence to the fact that what women say and how they say it is always up for debate, even if wrong. Women's speech will be policed until the end of time—and this policing will come from every possible angle.

"Like" must work against the pervasive myth that it is a meaningless word, a word that makes women sound dumb. This myth is hardly new; for years grammarians and prescriptivists alike have vehemently decried the word's "improper" use, letting it set an example of how society is going to hell in a handbasket, one "like, totally" at a time. In 2016, CNN published an article about this very subject, written by a concerned Kelly Wallace, who found herself confronted with her daughter's tendency toward this verbal tic. "Suddenly, I heard the word 'like' coming out of her mouth after every few words," she writes. "I cringed, but I also know there was nobody to blame but myself." After a bit of self-flagellation, Wallace turns to experts out of concern for her ten-year-old daughter's speech habits and what it might mean for the rest of her life. Sexism doesn't seem to be Wallace's end game, but the bulk of her concern is directed first at her daughter and then also at her daughter's peers. And, according to the various experts she consults in order to solve this problem, saying "like" so much is a weak stance that diminishes the meaning of the sentence in which it appears—and ostensibly the intelligence of the speaker using it.

In my research, I have yet to come across a study that draws a direct link between excessive—or any—use of the word "like" and intelligence. This, perhaps, is because there is no link at all, despite the hidden implications in Wallace's article and many others that using "like," like, a lot means anything at all. Language is an ever-evolving beast that, to paraphrase one of Silicon Valley's more embarrassing aphorisms, moves fast and breaks things. It is always changing, always iterating, and it is our responsibility to keep up. (It's worth noting that, in her book *Word by Word: The Secret Life of Dictionaries*, former associate editor for *Merriam-Webster* Kory Stamper notes that the smallest and shortest words often have the longest entries, precisely because of how complicated those tiny little words can be and how they change and morph over time.)

Somewhat unsurprisingly, nailing down a specific and all-encompassing definition of what language actually *is* is tricky. We can turn to the linguist and anthropologist Edward Sapir for a working definition: "Language is a purely human and non-instinctive method of communicating ideas, emotions, and desires by means of a system of voluntarily produced symbols." In short, language is the written variation of the words that you speak every day, but it's not just a means of relaying information. How we speak and what we say are intrinsically tied to where we're from. We can also look at language as a series of socially accepted rules put into practice, meant to deliver key context clues about where we come from and how we experience the world. It's also tied to race, class, and social standing; the way we talk and the words we use say a lot about where we come from. One person's "soda" is another person's "cola" (and god help you should you find yourself in the middle of an argument about it, because both sides make compelling points). Language is also performative by nature; when you choose the words you say, you're undergoing a series of imperceptible mental calculations that take into consideration the audience, what you *actually* mean, and, crucially, how you want to be seen.

A polite person's natural inclination is to adjust their manner of speaking depending on the situation and the audience—but sometimes proximity and environment lead the charge. If you spend a lot of time in a place where people speak differently from how you do, you will likely pick up some minor affectations—like a college sophomore doing a semester abroad in London and coming back talking about lifts, boots, and lorries. We change the way we speak and what we say to blend in or to make other people, and also ourselves, comfortable. This isn't a requirement for interpersonal communication, but it is sort of nice when it happens. It's considerate. It's kind. And sometimes, when it doesn't happen, it's extremely annoying. If, for example, your sister, who happens to be a lawyer, enters conversations with a seemingly pathological need to be right, the interactions that follow feel, at times, like a court of law. In this fictitious example, which is in no way based on any part of my life, what would be nice is if this sister dropped the cross-examination about my plans and why they don't coincide with her own, when all we're trying to do is discuss train tickets to go home. It's crucial to hear not just what the other person is saying but how they are saying it, to look within and fine-tune.

Politicians are remarkably adept at these mental gymnastics, knowing full well that the way they speak to their constituencies could sway public opinion in their favor. In 2022 Beto O'Rourke was in the middle of a campaign event in Texas, addressing a somber audience about the Uvalde school shooting, when a heckler in the crowd had the audacity to laugh. "It may be funny to you, motherfucker, but it's not funny to me," O'Rourke said, responding as if he were a stand-up comedian heckling a heckler and not a gubernatorial candidate in the great state of Texas. Intentional or otherwise, the meaning was clear: Beto O'Rourke wasn't just any old politician, slimy and self-serving—he was a person, too. Sarah Palin employed a similar kind of posturing during her disastrous run for public office, leaning on a folksy affect to appeal to a conservative base that seemed leery of the particular sort of change a Barack Obama presidency might bring about. Obama, of course, has a very distinctive way of speaking; it communicates humility and is stentorian without being overpowering or domineering. When he talks, you naturally want to listen, and his speech patterns are reflective of the cadence one might hear in a Black church. It's a distinctive manner of delivery that, honestly, only works for him, but bless Senator Jon Ossoff for trying. In his 2017 concession speech after his first run at a seat in the House, Ossoff seemed to be delivering a solid if not confusing Obama impersonation. Maybe this was because Obama conveys authority when he speaks, but for Ossoff, a millennial who came of age in the Obama era, that's just what a politician should sound like. Maybe he was trying to prove that he was just as serious as a young Obama was and had just as much potential. In all of these cases, the politician's use of the vernacular seemingly brought them closer to a mass audience. The use of this vernacular was not counterproductive but helpful. (Palin may not have fared well in the end, but this was because her speech revealed an actual ignorance of government instead of being a put-upon disguise that could be dispensed of at will.)

When I raise this point to Dr. Alexandra D'Arcy, a professor at the University of Victoria who has made much of her life's work studying the word "like," she helpfully clarifies this further. "What is the point in talking to the public if they can't understand your message?" she says. "And if you care about your message being shared, then you need to render it in a way that is legible to your audience." It's interesting to think about legibility in speech versus written communication, but it's a concept that handily applies to both. "Like," too, can be a simple and effective way to render a concept legible. Every time you throw a "like" into a story, whether it's recounting an argument or talking about the one thing your sister does that is always so annoying, you're sharpening a recollection, providing further context, or at least easing the reader or listener into learning more information. While, of course, having time to further organize your thoughts.

There are other words and phrases that perform similar functions and that sit alongside "like" as filler words that are, at first, written off as unnecessary. "I mean" and "you know" get thrown into sentences left and right and function as verbal pauses that allow the speaker to gather their thoughts or to link two seemingly disparate thoughts together. These phrases often appear in the same part of a sentence and therefore do very similar jobs, but "like" is a slippery little thing. Combine "like" with either of these filler phrases and, depending on where you place it in the sentence, the word puts in work. "Like, you know" and "you know, like" have two very different meanings. Both are provocative opening questions to a conversation hopefully full of very good gossip, but to me, the former implies seeking advice, and the latter, the opposite. "Like" functions as a free agent, slotting into a sentence that needs it with little fealty to how it appeared before and changing the meaning of what follows.

Contrary to the popular belief bandied about by its naysayers, "like" doesn't obscure meaning—it brings it into sharp relief. It facilitates context, an essential part of communication that so often goes overlooked. A simple question with an answer that is either surprising or a little embarrassing requires showing your work—you make a little map of how you got there in the first place. And "like" helps that process along, linking seemingly disparate thoughts or presenting a snapshot of how you feel about what you're saying rather than recounting what was actually said. Perhaps "like" functions as a means to highlight what felt true at the moment, because that context is as crucial to a story as what actually happened. You're allowing the listener a glimpse into not just what happened but how it made you feel. This isn't the oversharing that's indicative of an alarming lack of boundaries. It's just an acknowledgment that how you feel matters, and an open invitation for the listener to respond in kind—the emotional equivalent of "I'll show you mine if you show me yours."

What's even more remarkable about this word is its plasticity. "Like has not completed its grammaticalization," D'Arcy writes in her academic book on the subject, *Discourse-Pragmatic Variation in Context: Eight Hundred Years of LIKE*, before presenting a use case of the word that thrills me to my core. "There is anecdotal evidence that 'like' is beginning to function as an owner, signaling that this speaker is taking the floor." At its heart, "like" is a word that does a lot of emotional labor, but in this capacity, that is the sum of its parts. Telling a story about the man who has somehow grabbed what's left of your heart and refuses to let it go is an arduous task, depending on the audience. But if you launch into that story with a drawn out "liiiiike" that seemingly comes from the depths of your soul, that one word is a sigh of relief. It's setting the burden down, just for a minute. It's not going to make a scene, but it'd be great if you paid attention. (Stay tuned for an especially spicy example of this usage later in this book, when we see how it has made its way into the pop music parlance. . . .)

A "like" hones the point of a sentence. It's a neon sign that directs the listener to what's important in a conversation, gesturing toward the thing you should actually pay attention to. Conversations without it can feel unnatural and stilted, like having a friendly chat with AI or someone very studious in their attempt to be taken seriously. "I ate, like, ten pounds of mashed potatoes," I say through a haze of carbs and wine at Thanksgiving, understanding that my audience will know that I'm taking some liberties. There's no way in hell that I'd eat that many potatoes, but the "like" lets you know that that's how it felt. "My mother grounded me for, like, *six months* after she caught me cutting one class," I say to a friend, recounting a core memory that still irks me to this day, some twenty years later. The "like" suggests that the amount of time served is less relevant than the act itself: It's not important how long it actually was (technically, closer to three months, after my stepfather took pity on me) but how long it felt to me (an eternity). "Like" is an easy way of validating your own feelings in a way that is necessary rather than self-indulgent—a little blip of vulnerability that invites the other party to do the same.

It's not news that the bulk of the criticism surrounding the word is sexist. Never mind the fact that research shows men use the word just as much as women do. A 2021 study out of UCLA clarifies this assertion. The assumption is, of course, that women use fillers, including "like," far more than men do, in accordance with traditional gender roles. But because those roles are now becoming outdated, it stands to reason that maybe this has changed. The authors of the study analyzed interviews of Californian college students and the number of filler words used over the course of their conversations. Surprisingly, the research revealed an interesting truth: "Women surveyed used significantly *fewer* filler words than men." (Yes, the filler word that women preferred to use was "like," while men favored "yeah," but this is indicative of how social pressure affects our word choices—"like" still carries a whiff of the feminine, and so men, terrified of sounding like a lady, shy away.)

Overuse of the word is a nuance of communication that's largely tied to women and how they speak. But "dude," arguably the male equivalent, receives little to none of the vitriol reserved for its counterpart. "Dude" is just as versatile, and if you're clever, "like" and "dude" can function as the only spoken component of a conversation. ("Like!" has a different meaning than "Like . . .") Both can be used as verbal shorthand; there is an entire *SNL* skit where "dude" is the only word spoken, to relatively powerful effect. But "dude" is not just a word; it's a marketable concept for a particular way of life, and that's where the difference lies. Heritage wool brand Pendleton reissued its 1972 Westerley sweater as worn by The Dude in *The Big Lebowski*, thanks to a generation of consumers clamoring for the iconic garment and whatever ineffable cool was contained within. Merchandising opportunities of the sort for "like" simply don't exist, because "like" is a word that apparently signals stupidity rather than an affable dumb or cool, and the latter sells much better than the former.

Though the above appears to be true, like Whitney Houston once sang, I believe the children are our future. Ice Spice, a twenty-five-year-old rapper from the Bronx, released her debut EP *Like..?* in January 2023. Though none of the songs on the EP or its deluxe version—released a few months later—shares the title of the album, the album title itself is, as the young say, a mood. According to the Wikipedia entry for the album itself, *Like..?* is meant to be pronounced in "regional vernacular dialect" or, specifically, African American Vernacular English (AAVE). While I cannot personally testify to whether that assertion is accurate, what I can say is that Ice Spice's use of the word in this particular case is, unfortunately, iconic. Ice Spice was born in 2000 and therefore is of a generation so far removed from mine that their habits, traits, and particularities can feel alien and also make me feel extremely, irreversibly old. I don't know what the teens are doing these days, and I've come to the understanding that it is no longer my business to care. But Ice Spice has a particular zest for life that's worthy of celebration or, at least, closer consideration.

She embodies the recklessness that comes with youth, a devil-may-care attitude that is less obnoxious and more aspirational. If there's any sort of comparison to be drawn between "like" and "dude," the male equivalent of a word that is just as innocent, it's that Ice Spice is sitting on a massive opportunity to reclaim a word and shape it into a lifestyle rather than just a phrase.

We should all be so empowered to shake our ass in a deli or, if the spirit moves, to throw bands at Chanel as if it were our right, not a privilege. And *Like..?* in the hands of Ice Spice and her cohort is a call to arms.

Truthfully, the word's versatility is such that it makes little logical sense that anyone is upset about it at all. But discrediting this word just because it "sounds dumb" is shortsighted, rude, and, I'm sorry, just a little bit sexist. Language necessarily evolves with the culture—and culture, by and large, is driven forward by the young. The guardians of grammar are resistant to change, and teaching those old dogs any new tricks is difficult at best and impossible at worst. "Like" is a word that only gains power the more it's derided—as they say, there's no such thing as bad publicity. And at this point, perhaps attempting to fight it is futile; the word is fully ingrained in the speech of the youth but also of the soon-to-be old. I'm what they call an elder millennial, born in 1982, brushing the hem of middle age. "Like" is so much a part of my speech that I'm writing an entire book about it. And as my generation slowly puts the boomers out to pasture, the usage of "like" will soon be status quo. The tides are turning faster than I'd like. The path of least resistance is resigned acceptance—"like" is here to stay.

Chapter 1

# Like, What?

I am roughly the same age as Frank Zappa's "Valley Girl," a song he recorded with his then-fourteen-year-old daughter, Moon Unit. Technically, the song was meant to be an excoriation of Valley Girl culture, but sometimes the best laid plans go awry. Even though the song is over forty years old, the lyrics are almost timeless: "Like, oh my god! (Valley girl) / Like, totally! (Valley girl)."

Throughout the song, Moon Unit speaks in the patois of her environment, in language picked up from attending bar mitzvahs and hanging out with her friends at the Sherman Oaks Galleria—standard teenage activities that are also breeding grounds for new forms of culture. The Valley in question is the San Fernando, a wide-ranging area in the urban gloop of Los Angeles that is 260 miles of sprawling towns and communities, including Burbank, Glendale, Reseda, Sherman Oaks, and Calabasas, the ancestral home of America's most powerful dynasty, the Kardashians.

For the first half of its existence, the Valley was largely rural, home to ranches and farmland, and somewhat of a refuge for movie stars wanting to be at a distance from the hustle and bustle of Hollywood. In 1939 Clark Gable and Carole Lombard bought a twenty-acre ranch in Encino, complete with citrus groves, oat and alfalfa fields, and few neighbors. Lucille Ball and Desi Arnaz lived on Desilu, a Paul R. Williams–designed ranch in Chatsworth, and only moved when suburban sprawl started to threaten the peace and ease of country living. The area underwent a transformation in the beginning of the twentieth century, when the groundwork was laid for it to become America's biggest and most culturally important suburb.

The postwar era was when the Valley truly blossomed, as hundreds of veterans, home from the war, flocked to the Valley in droves and bought into the American Dream, thanks to the Federal Housing Administration (FHA) providing them with loans with long repayment periods, thereby helping them finance their dream homes and solving an affordable housing crisis in the process. Families—mostly white, thanks to racist and long-standing redlining tactics enacted by the FHA—moved to the suburbs and lived enchanted lives: two-car garages and swimming pools in the backyards, in neighborhoods where every house looked the same.

The San Fernando Valley certainly doesn't have a monopoly on the appeal of suburbs, but its strong hold on the idea of suburbia and its particular ennui in that part of the world has largely been thanks to popular culture. Unlike the suburbs of New York City, on Long Island and in the northern reaches of Westchester, the Valley enthralls because of its sheer size—miles and miles of single-family tract homes, as far as the eye can see. This sort of visual monotony is immortalized in Malvina Reynolds's "Little Boxes," a catchy lament for culture at the hands of tract housing and the middle class's conformist ideals—rows and rows of single-story ranch homes, one right next to the other, often arranged around a cul-de-sac, and mind-numbing in their sameness. (Famously, "Little Boxes" is the theme song to the Showtime series *Weeds*, set in Agrestic, a fictional, bleached-out town in the Valley, starring Mary-Louise Parker as a widow who sells weed to support her two sons and accidentally on purpose becomes a drug kingpin.)

What distinguishes the Valley from its other suburban counterparts, though, is its relative newness. Unlike the bedroom communities in the Tri-State area, the Valley is new(er). Fancy white people have been living in Rye, New York, a tony enclave with a very nice yacht club, since its establishment in 1660, drawn there by its proximity to Midtown, "good schools," and the Long Island Sound. The sense of history in the Valley is much more current and, therefore, slightly more interesting. Johns Cheever and Updike, as well as Richard Yates, immortalized the East Coast suburbs in their work, but the suburban ennui depicted in works like "The Swimmer," *Rabbit, Run*, and *Revolutionary Road* is WASPy and repressed and dark—the complete opposite of the Valley's relentless sun, strip malls, and inherent shoddy weirdness.

The look of the Valley and the customs of its inhabitants staked a foothold in the American imagination thanks to TV and film depictions of the area. Amy Heckerling's *Fast Times at Ridgemont High* is very much a movie about the Valley, as is

*Back to the Future*, which was shot in the area. The Brady Bunch live in an unnamed Los Angeles suburb in a house so suburban and iconic that in 2018 HGTV purchased it and, with the help of the original cast and some stars from their own stable, meticulously renovated the interior to replicate the set where the original show was shot. (In 2019 HGTV aired the results of this experiment in a four-part miniseries, *A Very Brady Renovation*, banking on the power of nostalgia.) In the Karate Kid franchise, Daniel LaRusso (Ralph Macchio) and Johnny Lawrence (William Zabka) launch an all-out karate war that starts at the All-Valley Under 18 Karate Tournament in 1984 and doesn't end until some forty years later, thanks to *Cobra Kai*, a sequel of sorts that is currently available on Netflix. Macchio and Zabka reprise their roles and play them with a heaviness, as if the weight of the Valley, midlife crises, and the karate championship that has eluded them both for so long are simply too much to bear.

For a time in the eighties and into the early nineties, the Valley dominated the popular imagination, driven by these films but also by another special place, where a teenager could find both community and an Orange Julius in the same day: the Sherman Oaks Galleria, the center of teenage mall culture and the birthplace of the Valley Girl.

In their attempt to poke fun at the girls who go to the mall to run up Daddy's AmEx, Frank Zappa and his daughter created the archetypal ditz: a shallow, fashion-forward teen with a particular manner of speech that was—and still is—coded as dumb. Valley Girls, like, buy shoes and clothes and, like, only care about themselves?

## Megan C. Reynolds

It's impossible not to read that sentence out loud in a very specific cadence: a touch of vocal fry here and there, and a pitter-patter rhythm that allows for a lot of syllables in every sentence, using many words to say not that much at all. The words lend themselves easily to this rhythm, and here "like" serves as a punctuation mark—a brief stop that allows the listener to understand how one thought relates to the next. There's nothing particularly offensive about this, especially if you're capable of expanding your way of thinking about language beyond what's "right." But in 1982 the Zappas' song struck a nerve, igniting a mini cultural moment.

"Valley Girl" was one of Zappa's only songs to crack the Billboard Hot 100, but other cultural exports from the Valley were doing the heavy lifting in sharing Valley culture with the masses. In 1983, some months after the song was released, *Valley Girl* debuted in theaters—a *Romeo and Juliet*-esque movie starring Nicolas Cage as a punk named Randy and Deborah Foreman as Julie, the ditzy blond from the Valley who loved him. Though none of the characters in Amy Heckerling's *Fast Times at Ridgemont High* exclusively identifies as a creature of the Valley, that movie introduced mall culture to a broad audience. And what was a mall in the early eighties but a stomping ground for Valley Girls and their cohort? In the Valley, superficial rich (white) girls talked, like, like this and, like, totally raised their voices at the ends of sentences, because, like, it's the only way to get people to listen? To aggravate them into paying attention?

It was only natural that Zappa's song inspired a brief wave

of books that capitalized on the popularity of this new way of speaking. *The Valley Girls' Guide to Life* is a work of humor written and illustrated by Mimi Pond, a cartoonist and artist who was living in New York at the height of the Valley Girl craze. "An editor from Dell Books called me up and asked me to lunch, and over lunch I was regaling him with stories about growing up in San Diego and being surrounded by stupid surfer dudes," Pond said—a veritable sea of Jeff Spicolis before Jeff Spicoli even existed. "He called me back a few days later and said, 'You know, we're thinking of doing a humor book about Valley Girls.' I said, 'What's that?' And he said, 'Well, there's a song out by Frank Zappa and his daughter. Have you heard it?' I bought the record; I didn't even have a record player. I had to go to a friend's house to listen to it once, and I went, 'Oh yeah, I can do that.'"

For research purposes, Pond returned to the West Coast and conducted a sort of ethnography of the girls in question by posting up at the Sherman Oaks Galleria and sniffing around. She eavesdropped on two girls on the escalator, bought them lunch, interviewed them, and then "trolled the beaches" and interviewed a few more. "I did the whole thing in, like, six weeks," she said. "And then it was on the bestseller's list, which was, you know, fantastic."

*The Valley Girls' Guide to Life* is absolutely a work of satire, in the same vein as *The Official Preppy Handbook* by Lisa Birnbach, but with a sharper tongue. (When documenting the mating rituals of the Valley Girl, Pond describes "ball-watching. That's when you stare at the dude's crotch to freak him out, then you go to your friend, you go, 'HOW DOES HE STACK IT?' real loud." This is one of the few *bon mots* from this work that I will take with me wherever life may lead.) Written in the voice of a Valley Girl, for an audience that both fears and admires them, *The Valley Girls' Guide to Life* is enlightening and even a little empowering, which was sort of Pond's intention.

"I mean, it was meant to be insulting to a certain kind of shallow teenage girl that they were making fun of, but it really spoke to a culture of teenage girls that hadn't really been spoken to before," she said. "And I wanted to defend them. Because they were girls and women, everything that they did and talked about was meaningless and horrible and stupid, you know, in the media and/or misogynistic culture in general. And I was like, I was there for them."

Even though the specifics of what's in and what's out have changed over time, if you squint, a teenage girl in 1982 is similar enough to a teenage girl now. When I asked Pond if she thought Valley Girls still existed or were antiquated, a thing of the past, she gently corrected me. "Oh, I think they do," she said. "I think I just kind of, like, zoomed in on this teenage girls zeitgeist."

Consider the small disquisition "On Makeup," in which an unnamed Valley Girl tells a brief but captivating tale about her friend Chrissie's foray into skincare, specifically placenta cream, a supposedly useful weapon in the interminable fight against old age.

"I go, 'EEWW, GROSS, you're going to put it on your FACE?' And she goes, 'Well, god, it's got protein, and it's for crow's feet.' So I go, 'How can you have crow's feet? You're only fifteen.'"

Chrissie's preemptive strike against the vagaries of old age is eerily similar to a more modern phenomenon occurring in the ranks of her contemporaries. Recently, Sephoras across the nation found themselves mobbed with hordes of tweens, the foot soldiers of Gen Alpha, clamoring for Drunk Elephant's Protini Polypeptide Cream (great for aging skin, restores firmness), retinol (excellent for skin cell turnover and will make you glow like a baby), and other beauty gloops—a trend credible enough to be covered by *The New Yorker*, the *Washington Post*, and *The Atlantic*. Naturally, influencers are to blame—tweens are watching beauty videos on YouTube and essentially mimicking what they see. Though I understand on an intellectual level that surely this frenzy has something to do with patriarchy, and therefore I should not pay it any mind, I have to say that the girlies are riveting. My perennial favorite, Evelyn, an icy blond tween who pats on moisturizer marketed to middle-aged women while rattling off a list of random things that bother her, is essentially a modern Valley Girl, and even if you don't like (or know) it, she's influencing the way you speak, just like her predecessors did.

Perhaps the most useful part of the book is the dictionary at the end—a compendium of anachronisms like "giving cone" ("Like, one of the grossest things you can ever do, it's, like, barfy just to even *think* about it, okay, like ORAL SEX, okay?") and "bitchen." Aside from those phrases, though, many of the slang included in the dictionary (and yes, "like" is in there, duh) have been absorbed into the way we speak now, and no one's really bothered!

Change is inevitable, and though the Valley Girl stereotype stuck around for a while, in 1995 Amy Heckerling did her best to subvert the narrative. Her film *Clueless* took the Valley Girl stereotype and introduced the idea that just because a woman talks like a total ditz doesn't mean that she's unintelligent or incapable of change.

When we first meet Alicia Silverstone's Cher Horowitz (Beverly Hills by address, Valley in speech and spirit), she's a feckless, superficial thing who treats shopping with reverence, cares very little about things outside of her small and cloistered world, and has a closet with technology so advanced that we still have yet to accurately replicate it. And, yes, for the majority of the movie, she's a bit of a lovable nightmare—a well-intentioned, very sweet teen whose guileless nature makes her the perfect target for her stepbrother, Josh (a young Paul Rudd, devastating, brooding, hot), whose undergrad nihilism belies a blossoming attraction to Cher that is ultimately reciprocated in a kiss set to swelling music that always grosses me out until I remember that they're fictional characters who are not related by blood. Cher's journey from self-absorbed sweetie to self-aware altruist is a fantastic example of the notion that the way women speak or carry themselves has little or nothing to do with their intelligence.

(I understand that much of this attitude smacks of late-1990s-to-early-2000s girl-power feminism and that we have moved past that point in the narrative, though probably not as far as we'd like.)

We can thank Cher and her cohort for their efforts toward mainstreaming the use of "like" in the vernacular, but it's unfair to blame her for its rise. The Valley Girls didn't start this particular fire—"like" in its many forms has been around for a good long time.

Taking a step back from, say, Frank Zappa and Cher Horowitz, we find that the word shows up in beatnik slang, including making an appearance in that beatnik urtext, Jack Kerouac's *On the Road*. Casual observers with a passing interest in this subject will likely pinpoint the word's slang origin here and leave it be. But this is misguided—almost everything we think of as new and innovative is generally just an iteration or continuation of something that's existed from time immemorial. In fact, "like" has been around since the 1750s. In Alexandra D'Arcy's book about the word, which reads as a scholarly and emphatic defense of its usage, she draws upon a rich and varied collection of corpora—collections of text or speech used to study language—to trace the actual history of the word, proving that "like" has been around for centuries, used very much in the same way we use it (and are chastised for) today. The sources are wide-ranging and comprehensive, from conversations with English teenagers in 1993 to the intriguingly named The Proceedings of the Old Bailey, a collection of court documents from London, starting in 1674 and ending in 1913. This is a particularly useful form of information, because unlike in much written language, where "like" and other filler words don't generally appear, scribes documenting court cases were writing down what they were hearing verbatim.

"Before the Valley Girls, it was used by the Beats; before the Beats, it was used by farmers in Northern England. Like, it's been around for a very long time. And there are really deep records of that," D'Arcy told me. "If you look at court documents from London, where you have scribes recording what witnesses are saying, it's there. So if it's showing up in use by a scribe, you know that it was part of the language for sure."

The corpora cited in D'Arcy's book reveal the use of "like" use across history and also borders and oceans: From New Zealand to Canada to the United States, people were using "like" in the same way, as a discourse marker like we do, like, every day. Consider this example:

"I almost felt like I was cheated, because I just, like, know how I'd act."

Divorced of any essential context, including the age and sex of the speaker, where the speaker is from, and whether they are still alive, this is a sentence that wouldn't sound out of place today, perhaps as a quote by an actor whose confidence balloon was popped when he didn't win the Academy Award he felt he deserved, therefore sparing the American public the diatribe on geopolitics he'd prepared instead of a speech. Naturally, you will only be a little bit surprised to learn that this sentence was uttered in 1865 by a ninety-year-old woman living on the West Coast of Canada.

"If the marker were a (North) American innovation, these examples and others like them would be inexplicable," D'Arcy writes. "The only possible explanation is that they are not innovative. They reflect a long-standing pragmatic strategy in English." "Like" is not an American phenomenon. It *is* English, but its proliferation through the English-speaking world is the work of empire. "We blame it on the Valley Girls," D'Arcy explains to me, "but they took advantage of a resource that was already available in the language."

In 1975, smack-dab in the jiggly middle between feminism's second and third wave, Robin Lakoff, a linguistics professor at University of California, Berkeley, published "Language and Woman's Place"—a meditation on the relationship between language and gender, viewed through feminism's clear lens. The central tenet of Lakoff's argument is that the way women speak expresses a lack of power and agency—that the language is weak and not strong, and that for a woman to be taken seriously, she must learn to speak like a man.

Lakoff writes about the doubling of identity that women endure on a daily basis, especially when it comes to their speech. "If a girl must learn two dialects, she becomes, in effect, a bilingual," she writes, explaining the natural shift that women and so many others make when adjusting the way they speak for their audiences.

An example: Lakoff identifies "tag questions" in women's speech—a little verbal hedge that sits between a statement and a yes-no question, used primarily in situations where the speaker isn't 100 percent confident that what they're saying is accurate or, better, true. A tag question allows a speaker to make a declarative statement but also gives them a tiny out. It takes some air out of the boldness of the claim, demonstrating a reluctance to just say what you mean and how you feel the first time without relying on or waiting for confirmation or validation from any other party.

"Did you feed the cat?" is a question that assumes that the addressee probably hasn't. Were I the one asking this question, the fact that I'm even asking in the first place probably means that the cat is yowling in a dusty corner of the kitchen, waiting for her kibble. But "You fed the cat, didn't you?" is an entirely different kettle of fish. If I'm asking someone a question in such a facetious manner, I'm expecting the answer to confirm what I already know—that the cat, again, is ravenous, wasting away, and will exact revenge for late dinner by taking an elegant, dignified shit next to, but not in, her litter box. Regardless of how I'm asking the question, I still want a response—using the tag question is less direct and therefore gives the addressee a possible out.

A tag question defangs a declarative statement by allowing the speaker to present as if they aren't really sure about what they said or how they feel, if only to avoid stepping on any toes. According to Lakoff, these kinds of tags are more often used by women, because communicating this way allows for noncommittal responses, thereby preventing conflict and keeping the peace. A hallmark of women's speech is accommodation—making others feel comfortable in conversations that are difficult or otherwise unpleasant. And the reason why women are so accommodating with their speech is because they were raised to speak like ladies, and men, on the other hand, were not.

Thankfully, we have largely moved past some of Lakoff's more quaint arguments about how women would be better off if they were more like men. And once you get past those, she makes some solid points. For Lakoff, these verbal tics are a defense mechanism—a preemptive apology in a situation that might not warrant it. None of the causes that come before or after the hedge are untrue to the speaker, but the hedge provides a little space for disagreement so as to avoid offense. Women have been socialized to provide and to facilitate, she argues, but, above all, to be polite. And politeness certainly doesn't include forcing your strident but correct opinions onto someone else without giving them a little space to disagree. (One could also argue that this method allows the speaker to dodge accountability, but rather, it's the opposite: By leaving a little space for uncertainty, you're acknowledging that you are human and therefore fallible.)

While feminism has enjoyed many small victories since Lakoff's article was published, there are still and will always be small fights to win. The ideas that Lakoff shares are nothing new under the sun: Women address feelings over facts, and men, the opposite. It's not that this binary is particularly bad, she argues, but both sexes should be able to access both sides of this equation with impunity. Simply put, we should all feel comfortable speaking from a place of feeling *or* fact, and we should be able to switch fluently between the two in conversation and, ideally, life.

While Lakoff is careful about coding any behavior as explicitly good or bad, the takeaway is clear: The way that men speak and carry themselves in the world is how women should try to be. Men prefer the tangible—facts and figures that they can grasp in their hands, like an eight-month-old baby figuring out object permanence. But women's speech is naturally client-facing—emotional and personal, giving the addressee the space they need to let down their guard. And unfortunately, we've been taught to associate vulnerability with weakness and to see empathy as being soft. The *implication* here is that men's speech is good and women's speech quite bad and in need of change to sound just a little bit more like men's.

This argument is one of the dusty ones that gets dragged out every time the usefulness of "like" is up for public debate. Well-meaning articles published in women's magazines and on the internet provide helpful tips for cutting filler words out of your speech, not because it makes you sound like a man but because it is stronger. Clearer. Somehow better. But what these arguments always miss is nuance. One word can have many different meanings, depending on where you put it, when, and why.

The generally accepted usage of the word is familiar enough to require little explanation, but for completists, I present a few examples:

I like garlic pumpernickel bagels. I dislike cooked carrots, bananas, most peas, broccoli stems, and when I reach into a bag of arugula and find a slimy bit at the bottom. I like the early morning, and I like running my errands on Sundays before 10:00 a.m. I would never associate with the likes of *those* people, Agatha, I mean, really. Doesn't that duck look a little bit like Aerosmith front man Steven Tyler? "He Hit Me (And It Felt Like a Kiss)."

Nothing to see here. No problems above! Were you to show these examples to your eleventh-grade English teacher with a kink for diagramming sentences, nothing would raise a flag. But when taken out of these contexts where the word is supposed to belong, "like" lives many other lives.

"Like" is a remarkably versatile filler word—a seemingly meaningless part of speech like "um" and "I mean" that appears plopped in the middle of sentences for no reason other than to let the speaker gather their thoughts and to show you how one disparate idea connects to the next. When you consider filler words and their general utility, you'll find that they come in handy for many activities, including but not limited to making you sound like a real human being in spoken communication. Eliminating filler words from some forms of speech is useful in certain contexts; one assumes that if you found yourself giving an impassioned speech at, say, the United Nations, you'd try to strike some of the bullshit from your speech—playing to the crowd in the hopes of achieving maximum results.

But eliminating filler words overall from spoken language is a narrow-minded and ultimately foolhardy line of reasoning. Language changes and evolves naturally, and like most other changes, big or small, it is futile to resist. To identify as a hazard or to try and eradicate a word that wiggles its way into—and fills the cracks in—the English language feels like time and energy better spent elsewhere. It's not like "like" is in any danger of ruining the next generation's speech patterns in such a deleterious way that they'd be risking a decent future, and if you don't believe me, simply look at some anecdotal evidence: I'm a woman who says "like" all the time, and unless I'm mistaken, that fact has not had a negative effect on my future. But the amount of fuss made over a word that is one of the most useful in the English language would make you think otherwise.

Consider its different lives outside of the realm of what's considered grammatically "correct." Linguists have identified four other ways the word is used outside of the adjective and the verb, both of which are commonly accepted and used so frequently that we don't even think about it. Of the four, two are closely associated with women and therefore are the most derided.

The quotative "like" is the one we blame on the Valley Girls but is now such a part of conversation that we don't really think about it at all. If you say, "I was like, 'What the fuck?'" as you relay a story about an irritating incident between you and your boss, chances are that you didn't actually say that—rather, that's how the interaction made you feel. "Like" in this context allows you to convey feeling rather than fact, and it fundamentally changed the way we tell stories—we no longer have to recite (or remember) precisely what was said.

"Like," as we have established, is also a discourse marker—a phrase or filler word that gives the speaker a moment to collect their thoughts and allows for a moment of hesitation. "I, like, didn't understand why that chair was so expensive, but it's, like, hideous and also incredible," one might say of a novelty armchair in the shape of a giant Pleaser heel that, for some reason, costs five thousand dollars. In this example, if you were to remove the "like" from the sentence, the meaning wouldn't change. It's a remarkably deft way to buy time while you're speaking, even if it's happening somewhat outside of your immediate awareness. Chances are, you don't pay any mind to this "like" in your regular speech unless someone makes it their job to point it out. While the quotative use of the word gets the most flak, it's these little verbal moments of respite, crammed into sentences that flow around them like a river over stone, that really get under people's skin.

As an adverb, "like" approximates value, time, or quantity, and has basically replaced "about"; there's nothing particularly glaring about this, and since it is generally used by men and women alike, no one really gets upset here. And finally, "like" is used as a discourse particle, which is similar to a discourse marker, but syntactically functions a bit differently. (A sentence can stand on its own without a discourse marker, which is generally found before or in between complete clauses.) When we use "like" as a discourse *particle*, though, it's meant to draw attention. Similar to the Bay Area's endemic intensifier, "hella," a "like" that asks you to pay attention is immensely helpful. If one of my sisters asks me what would happen if I, like, didn't answer the phone every single time our mother calls, the "like" here draws attention to the meat of this conversation: that my mother calls way too much and maybe, just maybe, it would be prudent to erect and then uphold a boundary around, like, my personal time and mental capacity to handle petty family drama.

When a single word is so useful, so beautifully flexible, and does so much with so very little, it seems illogical and short-sighted to disregard its importance. But lest you forget the sexism of it all, the word faces criticism because of its association with teenage girls. To be crystal: The evidence shows that the word's use in the vernacular is not strictly women's work and that men use it just as much, if not occasionally more often. And to be extra clear, none of these usages point toward anything close to weakness. In fact, using a word that's so linguistically dexterous is a sign of a particular kind of emotional intelligence that we could all stand to use more of.

If we revisit Robin Lakoff's assertion for a moment, weakness is a trait largely (and incorrectly) associated with women and is reinforced by the way they speak. In order for that perception to change, they could consider striking "like" and its pals from their vocabulary, perhaps so that they sound more like men. But part of the way young women use speech is to establish comfort and rapport and to strengthen or build relationships—the perceived weakness becomes a strength. In a 2023 op-ed in *The New York Times*, Dr. Adam Grant, an organizational psychologist at Wharton, wrote that there's actually some benefit to using "weak" language of the sort we generally associate with women, especially in the workplace—coincidentally, where women are told they must sound the strongest for success. When asking for a raise, women who used hedges and fillers were more likely to get it in part due to how they asked. Instead of barreling into a supervisor's office and demanding more money in a Jerry Maguire sort of fashion, women who padded their asks with linguistic Bubble Wrap appealed to their supervisor's sense of superiority—the way they posed the question allowed for their boss to maintain a position of power and avoided any hint of arrogance.

"That language doesn't reflect a lack of assertiveness or conviction," Grant writes. "Rather, it's a way to convey interpersonal sensitivity—interest in the people's perspectives—and that's why it's powerful."

It's hardly revelatory to admit that, more often than not, being nice to other people and actually giving a shit about their points of view are a pretty decent way to live and, if you're lucky, will net relatively positive results. It turns out that kindness isn't a weakness after all; empathy, just a dash, is a powerful bargaining chip. In serious conversation, too, there's nothing wrong with wanting to soften the blow. Not every situation requires a hammer. "Like" smooths the edges from strong, sharp, uncomfortable emotions, lowering the intensity until it feels more manageable. For those who don't love to be vulnerable and would rather eat glass than be the one to start and then have a difficult conversation, "like" is a tiny life raft bobbing around in a stormy sea.

# Interlude: The Grammar Wars

Language is dead when it only exists in books and is spoken by a dying population. Latin is the prime example of this: Even if you studied it in high school and had a Latin teacher who sort of made you speak it in the classroom (thank you, Mrs. Meyerson), its main purveyors are the functionaries who flit through the halls of the Vatican, attending to the pope. English, on the other hand, is very much alive—vibrating with life, full of energy, and changing in front of our noses at a rate so fast that it is impossible to accurately track. And because of this fact, which is one that applies to any living language, it's sort of difficult—if not impossible—to say definitively what's "right" and what's "wrong."

Arguing over who has the right to language and therefore how it should be used is an endless war between prescriptivists and descriptivists. Liberals and conservatives employ the "proper" use of language as a weapon on the political battleground. If you "care" about language in a way that clings to a fading past, then naturally its misuse gravely upsets you. John Simon, a legendary curmudgeon and longtime theater critic at *New York* magazine, was one such cultural figure, someone who absolutely thought that the English language was going to shit. Simon was a sharp-tongued man who rarely wrote a positive review and was fired from his job at *New York* in 2005—a position he had held, uninterrupted, since 1968. He died in 2019, presumably still believing that a heady combination of political movements (like the Students for a Democratic Society), diversity, and television were three major contributing factors to the downfall of the language. Squint and you'll see that this kind of hand-wringing is essentially a dog whistle for the Right. Prescriptivism is an inherently conservative trait, because it privileges the past and not the present or the future.

Prescriptivists are sticklers for rules, usually ones that have been set by some dusty old men in the past and have changed very little as time has gone on. Words have one meaning—the right one—and deviation from their "proper" usage is a sign of society's decline. An example: "Hopefully" is a word that, when used improperly, will make prescriptivists mad. Until I started research for this very book, I thought very little about how "hopefully" is used, but I learned very quickly that we're all using it wrong.

In their book *Origins of the Specious: Myths and Misconceptions of the English Language*, Patricia T. O'Conner, former *New York Times Book Review* editor, and her husband, Stewart Kellerman, do the work of dismantling commonly held myths about the origins of some words and phrases that we use every day. According to O'Conner and Kellerman, there's technically one correct way to use the word "hopefully," and that's as an adverb, modifying a verb (i.e., "I wish hopefully for a lobotomy."). The other use of this word, which you likely do every day without thinking about it, is this: "It's a hanging offense, the sticklers say, to use it to mean 'it is hoped' or 'let us hope. . . .' The word 'hopefully,' the argument goes, should modify a verb, not a whole sentence," they write. So, if you said, "Hopefully I don't throw up," that's wrong because, essentially, your desire to not toss your cookies in the potted plant over there is the thing that's being modified. (Acceptance for this use is widespread, O'Conner and Kellerman write, "because no other word does the job quite as well." Sounds familiar!)

If reading that example produces an immediate sense of irritation, then you understand precisely how specific, nitpicky, and annoying it can feel to be at the receiving end of this sort of irrelevant criticism. The implication, of course, is that using the word wrong means that *you* are wrong—uneducated, unintelligent, and not worthy of further consideration.

Descriptive linguistics, which emerged sometime in the 1960s, is prescriptivism's opposite. The motivation in this particular subfield is not punitive; rather, descriptive linguists just want to listen, to observe, and to document how the language is actually being used, without making any attempt to correct it to a set standard. In 1961, when *Webster's Third New International English Dictionary* was published, labels like "slang" and "colloquial" were dropped from definitions, essentially legitimizing a corresponding word's place in the canon of modern American English.

Language also serves as a shortcut to identity—the way we speak and the words we say are all intrinsically tied to where and how we were raised, and contribute to maintaining and upholding stereotypes that can often be damaging. Southern slang and New York City slang (as well as their respective accents) historically suggest stupidity or a lack of intelligence, but conversely, many people can't help but find them charming, too. (If this statement feels false or otherwise irrelevant, please think of the two shining examples in this space: Matthew McConaughey, whose accent makes even the most inane stonerisms sound profound, and Pete Davidson, a man with an outer-borough honk that has appealed to women like Kim Kardashian, Ariana Grande, and me.)

Grammar prescriptivists and the like are always wringing their hands over the closing gap between spoken language and written language, with the worry being that the way we speak (casual, informal, "wrong") will soon impinge on the written word—for worse, never better. For anyone who has ever sent a text message, it's clear that this is perhaps the only medium where the line between the two blurs to a mush. Stripped of important nonverbal cues that accompany verbal speech like body language, tone, eye contact, and general vibes, text language can be frustratingly vague or confusing. If you've ever been on the receiving end of a text that makes you gasp with how cruel it reads but are able to step back and hear how the same thing might *sound* in the context of your relationship with its sender, then you understand this better than others. We text how we speak but often could stand to be clearer in that particular medium, because quite often, without the tiny bits of humanity on display in in-person interactions, words can sound much, much harsher than they're meant to. (I think. Or so I've told myself at various times in an attempt to prove that it's true.)

But the real gatekeeper of the rules to acceptable speech is not some grumpy group of white men sitting in a literal tower somewhere, thumbing through ancient tomes to back up their arguments—it's the media.

Newspapers do a lot to maintain the standards of language, and our current twenty-four-hour news cycle requires the talking heads that populate MSNBC, CNN, Fox News, and the like to become adept at improvisation. When there are so many minutes of airtime to fill in between breaking news segments and weather reports, it's natural that news anchors will find ways to fill the space. Even though these people are in serious positions of power, the way they talk in these ad-libbed moments will always be more informal than how the same information would be conveyed in writing. This line-blurring doesn't mean that our ability to understand written English is declining; rather, we are adapting to change in real time, and any of these petty squabbles about right and wrong are merely bumps on the road to change.

American English changes frequently and easily, and it's this sort of change—rapid and unfettered—that generally freaks people out. So many of the words we use today are loanwords, borrowed from other languages and integrated into

American English—a result of a steady stream of immigrants over the course of centuries; certainly, that change was met with resistance, but now, where would we be without words like "kindergarten," "déjà vu," and "sushi"? This adaptability goes hand in hand with another cornerstone of American identity: our informal nature, which is remarkable and emblematic enough that international students coming to attend college in the US get a heads-up just so that they're fully prepared and know what to expect. "Partially due to their sense of equality, Americans tend to be very informal," reads a blog post on the University of California, San Francisco's website for international students. "Often Americans will ask, 'How's it going?' as a way of saying hello. While this informality can be startling if you are not used to it, Americans mean it as a warm and friendly gesture."

The foundational identity of the United States is one of constant and consistent reinvention. It makes sense that our language would change so quickly, as it is simply another facet of the uniquely American desire to innovate, to improve, and to forge a path ahead into the future. And crucially, we value speed and efficiency in our daily interactions—and "like" is arguably a shortcut for many things, which is in part why it's so useful.

## Chapter 2

# And *Then* I Was Like . . .

One evening during a summer when I was feeling particularly sad, a stranger peacefully broke into my home while I was asleep. An unfortunate series of circumstances led to this incident. The door to my bedroom was ajar just a crack so that the cat might have free passage between rooms without waking me up. My front door was *not* locked—I know, yes, I know, and it didn't happen again. I left the front door unlocked because, most likely, when I went to bed, I was stoned. This latter fact didn't prevent me from waking up to the sound of a man's voice whisper-shouting, "Sarah? Sarah?" from the depths of my very dark and rather long apartment.

I haven't a clue what I actually said, but my guess is that I yelled, "No? Who?" without getting out of bed. The sound of my voice, which belongs to Megan and not Sarah, was enough to flush the intruder out of my home and into the dark. Because I am great at going to sleep almost instantly after an event that would keep anyone else awake, I did just that. The next morning, I remembered the night's events as if they were a dream. The experience was not traumatic for me, mostly because I was not murdered in my bed, but also in part because I thought I'd imagined it for a good ten minutes when I woke up. I managed to convey this attitude to friends when I recounted the story, all of whom were aghast that I had fallen asleep with the door unlocked and also that I had not started screaming immediately upon hearing a strange man's voice in my apartment.

(The conclusion to this thrilling tale is that, supposedly, the man was attempting to visit my neighbor, who lives across the hall and is named Sarah. The explanation for this nocturnal visit feels spurious, but I'll let it slide: Allegedly, the man was a friend coming to check on Sarah, who was testing medication for a surgery, and he must've gotten the doors mixed up. Plausible, I suppose, but no hard feelings either way.)

One of life's inconsequential joys is telling a story about something traumatic, terrible, incredible, or terrifically irritating in front of a receptive, captive audience. Life is nothing more than a string of relatively boring incidents punctuated with moments of great sadness and ecstasy. When something happens that feels even somewhat remarkable, telling someone else about it temporarily relieves you of the burden of living with it yourself and, subsequently, the consequences of your decisions. The way we tell a good story that lands with our intended audience is generally to spice things up without straying from the truth. Some two years later, the contours of my break-in are fuzzy, if not completely erased. Even telling it to my friends when I did, hours after it had happened, I was unable to recite back the events exactly as they'd occurred— not because my short-term memory sucks, but because a blow-by-blow recounting of the truth is boring and that's not how stories should be told. There's a difference between a story and the truth, and "like" allows you to live in the space in between.

When you recount a story to a friend, it's often more important to convey how the incident made you *feel* rather than what actually, really happened. And as I learned from my conversation with Alexandra D'Arcy, the quotative, which is the newest and most innovative use of "like" in the vernacular, is also the most derided. But to me, and also to D'Arcy, it's by far the most interesting. "The short version is that 'like' has functioned with the verb 'to be' to introduce direct quotation in speech, because we don't really use it when we're writing fiction," she says. For a long stretch of the English language, "say" was really the only tool we had to convey speech in a story. As a tool, it's pretty utilitarian and very handy, but doesn't quite convey the showmanship of the breadth of spoken communication. If you say that someone said, "Why on earth are you always taking out the garbage and *not* putting a liner back in the can?," chances are they're not saying this calmly, because, from the sound of it, this is a repeat occurrence and should probably be remedied. But even if that person shouted or complained or screamed or bellowed or howled, in conversation it's always "said." "Like" offers another way in, allowing for the nuance that those other verbs would afford. "The simple story that has been told about 'like' is that it came in and replaced 'say,'" D'Arcy says. "But the complexity here is that 'say' can only do speech for us. But what happened in the quotative system in speech is that people started quoting way more than speech. And, in particular, they started quoting those internal states."

(This, for the record, is the stuff that makes people the angriest, for it makes little grammatical sense, and to a generation staring irrelevancy in the face and clinging to the now-outdated familiar, it's a baffling way to relay information.)

Some examples to consider: If you say in a story, "I was like, 'What the fuck?,'" one assumes that you probably didn't say that verbatim, but rather, that's how the incident made you feel. Historically, this shift occurred in the 1960s, so its use in this fashion is relatively new, but it's had a major impact on the way human beings communicate and therefore relate to each other. When "like" knocked "say" off its throne and entered mainstream speech, a remarkable shift occurred—the way we tell stories now is fundamentally different because we make space for feelings as well as facts.

The line between the two is often blurry; it doesn't always matter exactly what happened, but it is often more interesting to hear about how it made you feel at the time. "Like" endears the speaker to their addressee. It leaves a little room for interpretation but also for connection, communication, and the chance to feel seen and heard.

Establishing a connection isn't absolutely necessary for every spoken interaction you'll have in your life, but knowing how to do so is quite helpful, as connection is one of the cornerstones of healthy and effective communication that leaves both parties feeling somewhat satisfied or, at the very least, not in tears. When you care deeply for someone and have to tell them something important or scary or big about your own feelings, well, best of luck, and I hope your connection is as strong as you feel it is. As I have been told repeatedly by my well-intentioned therapist, feeling both seen and heard in a relationship has something to do with happiness. Yet being able to communicate effectively with the people we love the most is immeasurably difficult. Unfortunately, I'm here to report that there is another aspirational state of being that contributes to a life full of healthy, productive conversations: vulnerability.

Understanding what vulnerability *actually* means is a personal journey, and the path to that particular enlightenment is one that we must travel alone. Learning how to do this is messy work. It's often uncomfortable, and in general, no one loves discomfort and most would do anything to avoid it. However, should you seek a guide for this quixotic quest, Brené Brown, an affable Southern shame researcher with a fondness for statement necklaces, is as good a guide as any. For Brown, whose body of work features books, TED Talks, and a Netflix special that routinely makes me cry, being vulnerable is "uncertainty, risk, and emotional exposure." Vulnerability is something akin to a superpower that, if you can harness it and use it to your advantage, you, too, can live an authentic life. "Vulnerability is the center of difficult emotion, but it's also the birthplace of every positive emotion we need in our lives," she writes in *The Power of Vulnerability: Teachings on Authenticity, Connection, and Courage.* Seems useful, I agree, but getting there is truly the stuff of nightmares. However, it's very doable for anyone with enough time, gumption, and dedication to the cause, knowing full well that all the horrific emotional purging is necessary to achieve your ultimate goal: to live an authentic and joyful life.

But vulnerability is difficult because it requires the temerity to admit out loud that you have emotions and that they matter because they are yours—and then you must find the strength to share that information when it's required with someone you love. Though I have yet to reap the rewards of this particular process, I can see them waiting for me on the horizon. After an entire life spent running in the opposite direction from vulnerability and so terrified of just asking for what I want, I can admit that there's probably some value in this practice. If the icky, soft, and therapeutic connotations around vulnerability freak you out but you're still interested in living a good life, maybe consider a more dramatic approach: radical honesty, vulnerability's loud cousin who can't hold his liquor and routinely makes someone cry at Thanksgiving.

In 1997 a Texan psychotherapist named Brad Blanton published *Radical Honesty*: *How to Transform Your Life By Telling the Truth*, a self-help-cum-personal-philosophy that espouses the virtue of sharing authentically for yourself rather than lying sometimes to protect others and also yourself. Other books followed suit: *Radical Candor: Be a Kick-Ass Boss Without Losing Your Humanity* is radical honesty's corporate cousin but with a softer touch. Published in 2017 and written by Kim Scott, a former Silicon Valley CEO and executive coach, the book discusses radical candor as the sort of philosophy that argues for speaking your mind without being a dick. "Radical Candor really just means saying what you think while also giving a damn about the person you're saying it to," the Radical Candor website reads—a softer update to Blanton's radically honest approach to life, but tailored specifically to an audience that needs vulnerability the most: CEOs and other executives who may have a difficult time viewing their subordinates as their equals.

But before they were able to reach radical candor, those who wished to live a more enlightened existence worked with Blanton's more blunt philosophy. "Being Radically Honest means you tell the people in your life what you've done and plan to do, what you think, and what you feel," the website reads. "It's the kind of authentic sharing that creates the possibility of love, intimacy, aliveness, and action." As a life philosophy and mantra for generalized self-improvement, the concept is simple in practice: If you are able to share your authentic experience, from what you're thinking and feeling to what you will do in the moment and in the future, you will be free from the prison of your own mind. While the results of whatever this practice entails sounds great on paper, in practice, not so much.

A. J. Jacobs, a journalist and author who has made much of his life's work enduring various stunts for the sake of journalism, practiced radical honesty for a 2007 piece in *Esquire* and discovered, that while there was a specific kind of freedom to be found in being honest in situations where you'd otherwise lie, embodying Blanton's philosophy in everyday life wasn't actually practical or sustainable for the long haul. Taken one way, radical honesty is a spiritual rebrand of just being kind of an asshole. But there's something appealing to this approach, if only for the promise that by doing so, you will be free from the shackles of anxiety, fear, and self-doubt that plague us all because, as my therapist routinely reminds me, I am a human being and those feelings are all a part of the experience.

As Jacobs found when he met Blanton, there's something refreshing about being able to conduct an interview as a journalist without any of the profession's conventions. There's no need to beat around the bush, because if you practice radical honesty, no subject is off-limits, and your interviewee, in turn, can say whatever they want about whatever it is you just asked, and vice versa. Again—in theory—this sounds remarkably freeing, but what radical honesty misses are consequences. Part of being an adult means being able to take accountability for your actions. Sure, you can tell your best friend what you really think about their partner, leaving no stone unturned, but once you've gotten that off your chest, chances are there's a real mess that you'll also need to tidy up. Choosing this path isn't the easiest way out, but personal transformation is notoriously messy work. Live your life standing in your own truth and be ready to weather what comes your way in return.

I don't doubt that Blanton and his followers feel a specific sort of freedom by running their mouths, largely unfiltered, about everything under the sun. Certainly, giving yourself free rein to be an asshole in the name of spiritual enlightenment probably feels pretty revolutionary at first. But I think radical honesty really only works when practiced by the people for whom it is the only mode of communication: children. Children are naturally radically honest because they have yet to develop the filter that we generally use if we don't want other people to hate us. Part of this filter, naturally, includes lying—little white lies when necessary, in situations where the unvarnished truth doesn't need to be.

Blanton's theory shares some similarities with Immanuel Kant's categorical imperatives. A component of Kantian logic is the universality principle, which is one of the aforementioned imperatives—things that all people must do in order to live a moral life. The universality principle is as simple as it sounds: It's the idea that every person on earth should be able to do the same actions, which is fabulous in theory but much messier in practice. Lying, for example, is generally considered one of the most basic ethical violations and therefore the easiest to understand. If we lived our lives in accordance with Kantian logic, lying would be immoral, regardless of the circumstances that might warrant it. Telling the checkout person at the grocery store that you're having a great day when really, my goodness, you are not is immoral because the action is self-serving. By concealing your truth from the checkout person, who would rather do anything other than scan your twelve-pack of LaCroix, you're making it easier for both parties to complete that social transaction and move along with their lives. For Kant, self-serving acts, such as the one I just described, are not generalized or universal by nature—the lie I told to the cashier about how my day is going was born of an impulse to protect myself first, and so while I *think* I'm doing a small kindness to both parties, I'm really just making life easier for myself.

Thankfully, most people don't knowingly live their lives following Kantian logic, so we are able to go about our day-to-day without every social interaction becoming a land mine for feelings, emotions, and oversharing.

Consider "I'm fine," a phrase that falls out of my mouth frequently when I am quite the opposite. Never mind that I often say this between gritted teeth, squinting through the Vaseline-y scrim of dried tears on my glasses, as I make small talk with the man at the weed deli on the corner. There's no reason for him to know that right now I can't sleep for shit and have lost hours of my life to TikTok tarot readers as part of a curious midlife pivot toward spirituality. Call this the burden of being a woman, accommodating the needs of others by suppressing my own, or just being polite—this teensy lie allows the conversation, however brief it might be, to keep flowing. It eases the burden of interpersonal relationships, two short syllables at a time. Part of being a decent person is being able to accurately read a room. Most adults are equipped with this skill, as it is one of many in the junky tool kit they have at their disposal. (Whether they use it is another thing entirely.) It would behoove us all to exercise self-awareness as well as the awareness required to handle most social situations, but especially ones that could be uncomfortable.

In some ways, "like" supplanting "to be" in spoken conversation is an easy way of sidestepping all this complicated emotional bullshit—a verbal shortcut that allows the speaker to share just a little without baring it all. When we use "like" instead of "said," we're entering a pact with our conversational partner. Both parties know that the story that's about to unfold is just that—a small work of autofiction, imbued mostly with facts or, more specifically, the facts that truly matter.

All this work is unappetizing because, quite often, telling the truth about how you're feeling and clearing the stage for vulnerability feels uncomfortable, and no one likes that. But one of the many ways life plays us for a fool is this: Humans are wired for connectivity, to seek out connection and community. We are not solitary creatures, despite the pervasive myths of eternal bachelors, lone wolves, and spinsters content to eke out their days tending to a cat, a cup of tea, and years of unresolved trauma. And as I have been reminded countless times, one of the best ways to find the community we all seek is to learn how to be vulnerable—not just for others but for ourselves.

The use of "like" in this context, as a means of expressing our feelings and inner thoughts indirectly, allows us to share tiny bits of ourselves and our experiences with one another, to let someone in, all in service of healthy communication and a deeper, more long-lasting connection. It's an easy verbal shorthand that, in some ways, shows not how much you love someone but how much you like them instead—an action that is often more difficult (and just as important as love). But love is a choice that happens in very specific circumstances—we don't love everyone that we like, but ideally, you like the people you choose to love—and arguably, liking someone is much more difficult, a lifelong process that evolves over time. Figuring out what you like, how you like it, and why requires some of the same vulnerability that comes from any bid for connection, no matter how large or small.

To actually like someone means that you've taken enough stock of their particularities, measured them up against your own, and found something like harmony between the two. Love is the more significant feeling, celebrated culturally as the end-all, be-all for a successful partnership, but *liking* someone you love takes some work. It's perhaps a more difficult occurrence than loving them, ironically enough—what yucks my yum might not yuck yours! Your ick—a small-scale, low-key zap of discomfort when witnessing a behavior in a romantic partner—isn't something that your therapist or a well-meaning friend whose personal lodestar is *He's Just Not That Into You* would call a red flag. It's yet another piece of information for you to assess the strength of your likes and how these stack up against the depth of your love.

Watching a man stand on his tippy-toes to get a mug off a high shelf while wearing those no-show socks that look like ballet flats might not bother you. For me, this fictional scenario hits me with a wave of ick so strong that I can't possibly entertain the idea of sexual, emotional, or intellectual congress. But another man, who likes to play video games with the sound on while I read a book in the same room, who emerges from the shower with his hair inexplicably styled like Donald Trump Jr.'s, doesn't elicit the same bad vibe. Instead, I laugh, I am tolerant, and, distressingly, this behavior further endears me to his charms. I like this person enough to continue to love them, and god help me for it.

**Megan C. Reynolds**

If love in a relationship scores the big moments—a proposal, the birth of a child, something about home ownership—then like is the quiet Muzak in the background of the rest of it all. Why trod through life in the deafening silence of your own company when you can find someone you like enough to have by your side?

Friendship is an essential part of a healthy relationship, and as you may read in Instagram captions and self-help books alike, it's important to be friends with the person you're with. All over the world, brides and grooms are saying tearful vows about marrying their best friends, and the implication is that if you don't like this person at all, you're setting yourself up for disaster. Every relationship is a snowflake, so to even make this statement automatically is to set yourself up for failure. But some of the best and longest lasting relationships weather life's vicissitudes because both parties do actually like each other— and that care reflects itself in the way you speak to each other, in what you say and how you say it. Difficult conversations are made easier with a few crutches to lean on—being direct in these matters is enormously challenging, because sometimes it would be easier to just not address the elephant in the room, even if it's been there for years. If you need to tell your partner how badly they made you feel and you like them enough to do so in a way that will cause the least amount of harm, the indirectness of "like" is to your benefit as well as theirs. A sentence like "When you leave your nasty workout shorts directly in front of the hamper so that I then step on them every night without fail, I'm like, 'Are you kidding me with this?'" points at how the incident in question made you, the speaker, feel—as if the shorts in question exist merely to piss you off, and maybe what you actually say when you step on the stupid shorts is more colorful and unkind to your partner, who I assume you love.

We show care and affection with this imprecision. When recounting a miserable day at work or a fight with a family member that would require a flowchart to properly explain, it's rare to do so as if you are speaking to the authorities. Yes, it's (probably) in your best interest to tell the police exactly what happened to the best of your memory and to do so in a way that is less conversational and more formal and structured. But in everyday life, which is full of stories big, small, and mostly mundane, no one really wants to hear the specifics. I don't need to know who said what and how exactly they said it. What I'm interested in, though, in all of my personal relationships and beyond is sharing just enough: letting the other person know how I feel by saying what it was like rather than what it was.

Chapter 3

# Well, Like, I Just, I'm Not, Like, Sure . . .

In April 2024 Boston Dynamics put Atlas to bed for good. Of the products created by the company—a robotics firm based out of, yes, Boston—Atlas's earliest iteration was the most like the Terminator in appearance, but time had smoothed out its various lumps and bumps, and the result was that it looked a little bit more like Rosie from *The Jetsons*—humanoid, friendly enough, like something between a machine and a toy. Baby Atlas was a stocky, thick-thighed machine with exposed and clunky hydraulic joints, ambling through the world in the manner of a toddler, each step deliberate and slightly unsteady. Over time the robot has lost some of its bulk, the hydraulics have become more integrated with its carapace, and the legs, slimmed down, have taken on an insect-like quality. The technological glow-up over the years resulted in Atlas's final form, a top-heavy clunker balanced on delicate flamingo legs, resembling the AT-ST Walkers that terrorized the Ewoks in the Battle of Endor but on steroids—a horrifying physical representation of the police state. After nearly a decade, though, this version of Atlas is no more. Its sunset was announced in a three-minute-long memorial video on YouTube that charted its (d)evolution over the years.

The work has the feel of a bloopers reel, but the overall effect is to invoke the same fondness you might experience while watching baby videos of your adult children. Atlas is not a human, but its story suggests that it's something to that effect. A robot is a machine, prone to mechanical failure but generally expected to perform its tasks flawlessly and automatically; Atlas's life, to be sure, does not follow that of a machine, and it is full of the highs and lows of an ordinary human life. Atlas performs feats of dazzling and uncanny strength and dexterity, but Atlas also makes mistakes. And those brief moments of fallibility are far more compelling than any feat of to-be-expected robotic and superhuman strength. When Atlas takes a spill running across a balance beam and flings itself crotch-first into the ground, it rolls around clutching the space where its genitals might be, convulsing in pain. These are details that only become more unsettling as the robot's physical form changes and its behaviors start to take on a human quality. The robot dances. It falls. It "stubs its toe." And at the end of the video—and ostensibly its life—the robot takes a bow.

From the standpoint of a layperson—especially one who is terrified of robots like Atlas taking over the world in a real way, programmed to kill those who oppose the rule of its maker—Atlas biting the dust is good riddance to bad rubbish. But Boston Dynamics wasn't quite finished. Just a few days after

## Megan C. Reynolds

Atlas took its final bow, the company revealed an upgraded version in an ominous forty-second clip that, upon first viewing, felt like both an advertisement for and warning about the future.

The camera pans over a robot lying as if in Savasana at the end of a Vinyasa class, but instead of being in a warm room redolent of both palo santo and body odor, it is in what looks like a training facility for a machine army. From the way the robot is positioned on the ground and the behavior and movements we generally expect from things that are vaguely humanoid, the viewer assumes the robot will rise to its feet as any human with regular joints would: sitting, then standing to full attention. What transpires instead is far worse than even I could have imagined: Atlas rises to its feet by folding its legs backward over its body, like a Cirque du Soleil contortionist. Once the thing has found its footing, the nightmare persists: Its head, followed by its torso, swivels 180 degrees. Unlike its predecessor, the new Atlas has what looks very much like a face: a round circle, kitted out like a ring light, that shares some of the cartoonish and childlike qualities with the cheeky desk lamp from the Pixar logo. Atlas walks forward, then backward, then, with a smooth motion, its body orients itself. There's an imperceptible straightening of its posture; if the robot had shoulders, you'd imagine them rising once to meet the earlobes and then, with an exhale, settling back down. Atlas walks on-screen with a peppy determination, like a cartoon businessman with briefcase in hand, striding with purpose toward his next appointment.

What's so terrifying about Atlas is not just its dexterity—it's also its design, which, over time, has shifted just enough to make the robot feel less like a collection of parts and more like a very fancy children's toy. The overall shape feels similar to C-3PO, a Star Wars drone built like an old-fashioned man from the 1950s, with a triangular torso that tapers down to a wasp waist, set into slim but strong legs. Atlas 2.0 will come equipped with Boston Dynamics's AI and machine-learning technology. They're meant to be used for tasks that human beings would rather not do—the dirty or dangerous or boring jobs, all of which *can* be performed by people for money. But why bother with the messy work of managing people when you can use a machine to get the job done perfectly every single time?

Robots, even those equipped with AI technology, will never actually take the place of human beings, though I wonder if by making a statement as declarative as this, I am willing it into existence. A robot might be able to move like a human being, but at the end of the day, it's very much a robot. And by the time the robots start to actually look like humans, so much so that we cannot tell them apart from the rest—well, I hope the fires will have come for me by then. (If you're interested, a fully realized vision of what this future might look like lies in Ronald D. Moore's *Battlestar Galactica*, where the robots do look like people and they are dead set on killing them all.) I feel confident that this version of the future is so far in the distance that we won't be around to see it. But looking like a human being, even if not a very convincing one, is just a part of it. If the robots of the future really do look like the rest of us, then they'll have to sound like us, too. And the way AI chatbots like

**Megan C. Reynolds**

ChatGPT and Google's Gemini do their best to sound human offers a chilling glimpse into the future.

 On May 2, 2023, the Writers Guild of America went on strike as the result of failed contract negotiations that started in March of that year. Writers were lobbying for better pay, staffing requirements, and, crucially, better protection (or any at all) from AI job interference. The contract, which was signed that September, after the industry essentially ground to a halt, didn't ban AI outright, but it installed some pretty strong guardrails. Studios could not use AI to write or edit scripts that had been written by an actual human writer, nor could they use anything generated by AI as source material for writers to then adapt into a screenplay. In short: The writing part of the movie industry was still firmly in the hands of real people, and that is where it will stay. The SAG-AFTRA strike, which occurred concurrently with the WGA's, also addressed AI interference, especially when it came to the role of background actors, which can easily be replaced by AI. In November of the same year, *Sports Illustrated*, once a magazine and now a website, was found to be using AI-generated writers for their product reviews, which, one assumes, were also written by AI. (If you're wondering why venerable sports publications like *Sports Illustrated* run product reviews in the first place, the answer is because many executives believe that affiliate marketing and e-commerce are effective strategies for making any sort of money in media.)

 Maybe this is the genesis of my chagrin: ChatGPT, Atlas, and other tech designed to emulate the touch and feel of a real person are just harbingers of a future in which any creative output is outsourced to a machine so sophisticated that we won't be able to tell the difference.

Despite the obvious and alarming implications AI software and machine learning carry, ChatGPT is a tool that can occasionally be useful. Embarrassingly, ChatGPT is a useful starting point for guidance in interpersonal situations that you've already talked through to death with every single one of your friends and anyone who will listen, so much so that by now the opinions of others have merged with your own. When a situation calls for true impartiality, AI is a neutral party with no skin in the game. If you ever find yourself in a position where you desperately and immediately need a list of suggestions on how to set and uphold boundaries, ChatGPT will deliver, providing useful information that answers the prompt in an objective manner. The results are serviceable and delivered in a tone devoid of personality or opinion. The same conversation with a caring friend would be inherently different; try as they might, friends have a hard time remaining neutral or completely objective in situations where you are struggling, and that's because they're your friends and they love you. Emotional situations require a delicate touch; this is a scenario in which AI's hall-monitor vibes are much appreciated. But ascribing any personality to the technology's output isn't right—a chatbot can't have a voice because a voice, and essentially a point of view, requires human intelligence in any amount, no matter how small. AI will always sound like a narc, even if the prompt in question is designed to trick it into sounding like a human being.

To test this theory, I spent some time mucking around with

**Megan C. Reynolds**

Gemini, Google's AI chatbot. The technology functions like any other: enter a prompt, wait a few seconds, and the machine spits out an answer faster than it would've taken you to ask the question out loud. One of AI's many touted benefits is its ability to break down complicated concepts in a matter of seconds. If you want to understand how an air conditioner works, as I did one afternoon, Gemini will explain it to you in the voice of an engineer, breaking down the key concepts in an easy-to-parse bulleted list—boring, sure, but useful. In an attempt to test the bounds of the machine's creativity, I prompted it to write a villanelle about my cat, Daisy, and the result was far better than anything I could come up with on my own. (Note that this isn't a particular victory for AI but a personal failure for me, as I actually didn't know what a villanelle was until I asked. Had I written my own to compare, though, my result would've been much better. Trust me.)

If you look at AI like it's a very sophisticated video game, then the future becomes a fraction less frightening. But my interest lies within its ability to sound truly human. What could I do to trick the chatbot into sounding like a convincing-enough person with thoughts, feelings, and emotions? I turned my attention to matters of the heart, since romantic relationships are (supposedly) the most rewarding but also most difficult relationships that exist, and ending them in a way that doesn't do anyone unnecessary damage is tricky. When I asked Gemini to write an amicable breakup email, the result was still clinical and detached, but ultimately, it was kind—not too far off from the way the energy between former lovers shifts abruptly from intimate and familiar to businesslike and brusque. I wouldn't use the script verbatim, but it's a decent thought-starter and a useful way of seeing your garbled thoughts organized in a format that's stripped of any raw emotion. When I read it out loud, it was clear that Gemini ingested and shaped the blandishments provided by the internet and presented a result so measured, mature, and calm that I'd be gobsmacked and slightly suspicious of anyone who spoke like this when breaking someone's heart.

This tone and general effect were not what I desired—if the forthcoming argument in favor of AI in the creative industry is that the work it produces sounds human enough, I was determined to figure out the secret to making AI sound real. And it turns out that if you ask AI to write a breakup email in the voice of a teenage girl, the result you get sounds a lot more realistic, albeit still unsettling and not quite right. "I know we promised to be each other's forever person, but lately 'forever' feels like a long time," it reads. "I'm starting to realize that maybe our forevers are headed in different directions."

God bless the imaginary teen who sounds this cool, collected, and mature when handling heartbreak; I imagine the teens these days are, in their own parlance, built different, and so maybe they are capable of even a whiff of this maturity. And this script was closer to the results I desired. Granted, this was an email and not spoken dialogue, but I still yearned for a hint of verisimilitude in the results. While I'm sure there are young adults so self-possessed and confident in their decisions that they actually would speak this way, I assume there's a wide swath of the population that assuredly would not.

## Megan C. Reynolds

When I asked Gemini to perform the same tasks but in the voice of a Valley Girl, I finally got the result I was after:

"Don't get me wrong, you're, like, the sweetest, most [positive adjectives about ex] dude ever, ever! But lately, I've been feeling, like, totally out of sync with, like, where we're headed. It's not you, boo, it's me! I need to focus on, like, discovering my own path and, like, totally blossoming into the best version of myself."

You can almost hear the uptalk in the sentences, rising at the end of each statement. Regardless, in the words of Whitney Houston, it's not right, but it's okay: This result is the closest by far to sounding like a real person, even though the tone of the messaging is so cheerful that it skews Pollyanna and sounds a bit like an alien who learned English by watching reality TV. My experiment sort of worked: When I set about on this unscientific test, my intent was to basically force the machine to sound human in a situation that required a gentle touch and a shred of humanity. And I was only able to achieve a satisfactory result after I asked the machine to do a stereotype. What made the Valley-tinged breakup letter sound even the teensiest bit human was "like," sprinkled liberally throughout, doing work in spaces that may have felt negligible at first but were actually very important.

When "like" is the thread that runs through a conversation or even a sentence, appearing in places where it technically doesn't "belong," it's a discourse marker—a word or phrase that fills the space between words, clauses, and independent thoughts in sentences. All discourse markers are grammatically optional; they don't change the meaning of a sentence and are technically extraneous bits of chatter crammed into our speech, with no immediately recognizable purpose. Essentially, they are filler words, and if you're able to divorce yourself from the negative connotations associated with them, you'll see how nicely they facilitate the flow of conversation and that they are therefore extremely important to effective communication.

Discourse markers like "you know," "I mean," and "so" are what we're taught to filter out of our speech to sound more authoritative, more secure, and, overall, more powerful, despite how useful they are. "Just because filler words are fairly common in everyday speech does not mean that they are useful," reads a schoolmarmish blog post published on the Harvard Extension School's blog in 2012. "In fact, they often detract from the listener's ability to understand a particular message."

And, yes, it's true that at first listen, hearing someone use those words frequently suggests an imprecise and therefore careless approach to communication. If we're filling our sentences with words that mean nothing, why are we talking at all? But when "like" is deployed in this fashion, it has many context-dependent meanings. "Like" forces you to pay closer attention to what's being said by making you listen for the how. It draws attention and pulls focus. And sometimes it's an easy and kind way to give yourself (and the person you're with) the space you need to say what you mean, even when you're not quite sure how to say it. Taking another person's feelings into consideration while also protecting your own requires the ability to accurately read the room. This is a uniquely human trait that separates man from machine. Discourse markers aid conversation—and we only know if the flow needs to be addressed in the first place because we have even a modicum of the emotional intelligence required to do so.

At its heart, communication is just a sophisticated way to translate the laborious work of having feelings into a format that makes sense to someone else. Learning how to do it well, if at all, is a lifelong task; ideally, we will all eventually have the wherewithal required to talk about feelings with confidence rather than uncertainty. But uncertainty is one of the more irritating foundations of regular life—there are very few things in this world that are guarantees, and most everything else is unknowable. I've been informed that getting comfortable with that concept is helpful for living a life absent of any self-imposed stress, but getting there takes time and also is a gnarly process. Filler words are the little helpers we rely on in conversations to communicate this ineffable sense of the unknown—sometimes we're, like, not sure what we want to say next and don't want you to, like, feel bad about what's being said now. A "like" gives you some space to ease emotional discomfort or, in some cases, allows you to buy time so that you're absolutely sure of what you're going to say next. It is this tiny act of kindness that AI will never be able to accurately replicate, because, thankfully, machines are not yet capable of feeling emotions.

In 2002 linguistics professor Muffy E. A. Siegel observed her then-fourteen-year-old daughter's speech patterns and wrote up her findings in a paper published in the *Journal of Semantics*. She homes in on the rampant use of "like" as a discourse marker within the very subset of the population that takes the blame for its rise: teenage girls. The most interesting function she found in her studies was this: "'Like' is one of the English language's most useful and adaptable hedges," giving the speaker the space to be wrong but also to gather their thoughts in real time.

A hedge is a remarkably useful tool for self-protection, and that need isn't limited to the young or supposedly vapid. But insecurity about one's thoughts, emotions, or actions is a trait largely associated with young women. And according to Siegel's findings, among the teenagers she studied it did seem like the girls were using it more than the boys. The reason that may be significant is this: Using hedges in your speech doesn't necessarily indicate a lack of confidence, but it *could* mean that you're not thinking before you speak. Despite the general advice that urges forethought, a lack of it isn't always negative. I'd say it depends on the nature of the conversation, the audience, and, broadly, the vibe at hand. For every time you've stumbled through a conversation when saying what you wanted was tremendously difficult, there are hundreds of others across your life when it wasn't. And if you were to revisit any example of those conversations with perfect recall, I imagine you'd hear "like" in a lot of different ways, serving the same purpose.

Formal speech of the sort one might employ in a TED Talk or a speech at the UN is generally preplanned. Even if the nature of the speech is casual and the setting informal, the speech itself is generally structured, with clearly-defined talking points, a thrilling climax, and a poignant or otherwise powerful denouement. Effective communication is clear communication, and so one would think that filling the liminal spaces between sentences or thoughts with words that don't matter would muddle the meaning. But any hedge or filler words used in public speaking are calculated additions used to convey a sense of familiarity and intimacy that's often unearned—to engender trust, to win over an audience, to get them on your side.

Politicians innately understand how truly effective their words can be and are quite adept at this trick. From the campaign trail all the way to the White House, relatability and—effectively—likability can make or break their futures. One Sunday in the summer of 2024, mere months before the presidential election, President Joe Biden dropped out of the race, thrusting Vice President Kamala Harris into a horrible fate—competing for the attention of the nation's voters with Donald Trump. Shortly after Harris was officially nominated, pop singer Charli XCX tweeted, "kamala IS brat," a clever bit of self-promo for Charli's album *BRAT* and also a nice PR moment for the Harris campaign. By Monday morning, the official X (the artist formerly known as Twitter) page for the Harris campaign changed its imagery to look like the cover of Charli's album—a green that hovers between snot and neon with blurry, lowercase, sans-serif font that read "kamala hq." Brat, for the record, is a lifestyle, based around someone whose preferred everyday look is "a pack of cigs, a Bic lighter, and a strappy white top with no bra," as Charli put it on the BBC podcast *Sidetracked with Annie and Nick*. (This is also my personal summer aesthetic and has been for some time, but I will let the children have it.)

Brat is rebellious in a way that any politician is definitively *not*, and brat is also a movement, I think, for those young enough to glom on to Y2K fashion trends and general attitudes in part because they were not alive the first time around. While I am all for politicians letting the masks slip for a sec to show slivers of their private personalities, it's preferable for me if they are generally not messy bitches who love drama. (Please think of the politicians who are messy bitches who love drama. How did we fare under that reign?)

To be clear—in any understanding of the word, Kamala Harris is not brat. But the savvy people on her social media team understood that they had an opportunity here, and so if pandering to a wide swath of voting-age people by tapping into a zeitgeist was their chance, so be it. For a period of weeks, it seemed like the only thing that existed on social media were memes of some of Harris's more notable quotables, like the one about falling out of a coconut tree, and the other, a stonerism uttered by a sober woman, about existing in the context of which we live in and what came before. (These nuggets of wisdom technically came from Harris's mother, but who's counting?) Remixes featuring Harris's distinctive, ebullient laugh, the coconut tree line, etc., proliferated on TikTok and elsewhere. I watched every single one, giddy off the high of feeling something akin to hope.

Piggybacking off a famous person's seeming endorsement and parlaying that in an attempt to reach young voters is not new; politicians do this all the time, and it is generally very uncomfortable for all parties. We have absolutely been here before—please think back to 2016, when Hillary Clinton's campaign merch included a shirt that said "Yaaas, Hillary!" and much of the campaign's burgeoning social media strategy included

Snapchat and Bitmoji. As Amanda Hess wrote in *Slate* in 2015, "IRL, Hillary Clinton is a 68-year-old grandparent who pronounces Beyoncé '*Bay*-oncé.' Online, she speaks the language of a millennial fangirl on all the relevant apps."

But in this case, for Harris, riding the brat wave until its natural end was a smart move. "It shows a recognition of how critical young voters are to winning in November, and a commitment to meeting them where they are," Gevin Reynolds, a former speechwriter for Harris, told *The Guardian* in 2024. In short, getting on the level of the audience you hope to win over is easier now, but it can also be paramount to your campaign's success. There is no way real way to measure the efficacy of Harris's brat era. A viral video of a group of men in the Fire Island Pines wearing brat-green crop tops that read "kamala" circulated swiftly after the announcement, proving in some part that Harris's whole thing was resonating. It is hard to picture a group of men waiting for the ferry in the Pines wearing crop tops for any other political candidate, except for maybe Marianne Williamson, who is so kooky as to be camp.

The Harris campaign's brat era was short-lived, but the real secret weapon on this ticket was Harris's running mate, Tim Walz, the affable and progressive governor of Minnesota, whose folksy, down-home affect could read a bit like pandering if it didn't seem to be so authentic and real. Harris, for all her strengths, is a tiny bit weird—not weird like Marianne Williamson—and that weirdness might be off-putting for some. But Walz's vibe feels real—he speaks like a normal person in a way that can be refreshing and occasionally disarming, depending on the context. During the vice presidential debate against the noxious J. D. Vance, Walz stumbled a bit through parts of the discussion about foreign affairs but rose to the occasion when speaking about abortion—completely relatable to the average person watching, who might find some sympathy for this man's position. Walz's tendency to talk like a normal person, with the same sort of unintentionally inaccurate statements that we all make about events in our past, is relatable, too. Notably, before the debate, the hubbub around his factually incorrect statement about being in Tiananmen Square in Beijing at the time of the massacre came to a head—Walz admitted that he was a "knucklehead" after being asked to explain himself at the debate, but dodged answering the question. "Instead, he seemed to slink away from an uncomfortable line of questioning by suggesting that his time in China later in the summer of the Tiananmen protests had informed his theory of American democracy" reads a debate recap from *The New York Times*. I'm not a candidate for political office and never will be, but I imagine if called out on a national stage about the veracity of a story with details I find to be irrelevant, I would quibble, dodge, evade, and then finally, as Walz did, admit my error.

Aside from this misstep, though, the general attitude toward Walz is that his folksy, down-to-earth manner is both a part of his actual personality and a way to appeal to voters who still love their guns but are starting to change their minds about Trump. (Walz was previously an ardent defender of gun rights, so much so that the National Rifle Association gave him an A rating, but that has since changed; it is now a solid F.) Speaking in an appearance on *Pod Save America*, Walz said that in high school, in rural Minnesota, he'd store his shotgun in his car so that he could go pheasant hunting after school. This anecdote is relatable because it is ripped from the pages of his lived experience—and it likely mirrors the experiences of thousands of other voters who may be undecided enough to lean left.

Harris, Walz, and other politicians are extreme examples of how we change our speech, both in content and execution, based on where we are, whom we're speaking to, and what the nature of the conversation really is. In Harris's and Walz's cases, the change is largely organic or positive—say what you will about brat Kamala, but it had *some* sort of impact, and Walz's entire thing is that he is who he is, whether you like it or not. But for a brief example of how this can play out negatively, think about the regular Joe Six-Pack American drag Sarah Palin, a blast from the past, adopted for her time on the campaign trail and how that entire persona is really just a hedge writ large. For example: If faced with a question about something you don't know about, like foreign policy, and you have to answer this question on national television, it is probably easier to try to talk your way out of it as best you can. When Charles Gibson asked Palin what, if anything, Alaska's physical proximity to Russia had to do with *her* knowledge of foreign policy, she replied, "They're our next-door neighbors, and you can actually see Russia from land here in Alaska."

Note that Palin's answer barely addressed Gibson's question and instead rephrased his question into a statement that wasn't ridiculous as much as it was very clear that she had not done her homework and was trying to bullshit her way in and around it. What else is a hedge than a way to dodge accountability when you need to?

Everyone values direct communication, but so many of us are incredibly terrible at it in practice—saying what you want to say is hard, and most of us are ill-prepared to sit in the uncomfortable aftermath of a blunt or otherwise upsetting conversation without immediately jumping to our own defense. Direct, powerful, forceful communication is ideal for a professional setting and objectively incorrect for conversations of a personal matter. I find it impressive if anyone can muster the strength to tell someone they love them in just one sentence instead of five or six, but that's a skill that comes with confidence—both in your own feelings and the possibility of reciprocation. Personally, I think life is a little more exciting when you know that about half the people you encounter will be absolutely terrible at sharing their feelings. This will make your own mediocre skill set in this particular area shine in comparison. We live, we laugh, we love, we learn. And the more you muddle through life putting to use the lessons of the past, the more you get better at the shit that makes you feel like shit. I cannot testify to this experience personally, as I have yet to reach a place where vulnerability is routine—I'm doing my best, I swear. But ten points to me and the rest of the world, for there seems to be a mutual understanding that sometimes a hedge is the kindest thing you can do for someone else, but also for yourself.

Allowing yourself the grace to make a mistake or to gather your thoughts on your own time is a nice way of putting yourself first while also taking someone else's feelings into consideration. It's not emotional labor to be mindful of someone else's feelings; it is simply being human. And the "likes" that you use to fill the space in between thoughts, when used properly, makes your speech sound like that of a person and not AI. What distinguishes a person's use of "like" from that of a particularly intelligent and well-trained chatbot is being able to take the emotional temperature of a conversation and adjust in kind—to intuit what could or could not be appropriate in a situation and, if you're lucky, to say or do the right thing. And arguably, it's this tiny shred of humanity that allows for effective communication and connection—despite what movies like Spike Jonze's *Her* depict, a machine is not a long-term solution for the problem of loneliness, no matter how human-esque it sounds.

(The general discourse around the equitable division of emotional labor in relationships seems to be that women do more of it, all the time, and they're tired. While that may be true for some relationships, I wouldn't say it's true for all. So to avoid making a generalization about love, a complex bouillabaisse of feelings and particularities that is unique to the two people in it, I'm not going to call this a woman's issue. It's a people issue across the board.)

It should be clear by now that artificial intelligence, no matter how sophisticated the algorithms become, will always struggle just a touch with sounding like a person with opinions, thoughts, and genuine, messy feelings. Alexa will never materialize into a real person, but she's an idealized version of something real—a helpful, patient, and all-knowing partner who won't get mad at you if you ask about the weather ten times in a row. And, if you will trust me on this journey, I think we should venture into the heart of another form of alternate, augmented reality: the messy land of reality-dating TV, where effective communication and a strong connection are requirements for success, marriage is of paramount importance, and the very human people thrust into this engineered reality are messy. Accountability, a vital part of this whole mess, is even harder to come by in these scenarios, because reality-dating TV gamifies the idea of love while also reinforcing the fairy-tale narrative that says marriage is the end-all, be-all. And watching the participants fumble toward an understanding about love is to hear speech simply riddled with hedges, because most of these people don't know how they feel about each other and, in one case, have not even laid eyes on each other before getting engaged to be married.

In this specific media landscape, it becomes evident that there really is a lid for every pot. On *90 Day Fiancé* and its various spin-offs, green-card marriages that are purportedly for love unravel in spectacular, messy fashion. *Love After Lockup* features recently released incarcerated people and their partners and follows them through basically what the title of the show says. *The Bachelor*, a television franchise old enough to legally drink, feels retrograde but still makes for very good TV, if watching young people who are often stupid conform to a rom-com-specific vision of true love is your idea of a good time. Countless other dating shows feature farmers, MILFs, twins, and fuckboys, and the one thing they all have in common is this: Everyone is desperate for the kind of love that only blossoms out of vulnerability and communication, and in many cases, every person participating is incapable of either, even if the object of their affection is truly right in front of their face.

Reality-dating TV is not my preference—competition-based reality shows where people have to do stuff is ideal—but I make exceptions for outstanding offerings in the genre. Netflix's *Love Is Blind* makes the cut. Billed as a social experiment, the show features hosts Nick Lachey (the former Mr. Jessica Simpson) and his wife, Vanessa Minnillo Lachey, as they guide a group of slightly panicked straight people of marrying age (early twenties to early thirties) toward commitment via an unconventional method. The show endeavors to answer the question posed by its title. Each contestant is allowed to "meet" their potential spouse by voice only, speaking to each other through the wall of one of the pods, a capsule-hotel-style windowless bunker plunked down on a soundstage and furnished like a middling Airbnb. Over the course of two weeks, the contestants essentially date around like you might in real life, all ten men and ten women piddling in the same very small pool. This process is harrowing for many reasons, primarily because it is wild to watch what looks like actual romance develop in a vacuum.

Honestly, I watched the first season of the show in the prepandemic winter of 2020, in the grips of a spot of sadness and also out of professional obligation. Being even temporarily sad about love and watching a show like *Love Is Blind* would maybe buoy some people's spirits—*if these clowns can find love, then there's hope for me yet!* For me, unfortunately, it had the opposite effect. I couldn't really tell you what happened in any of the episodes I watched in order to review the show for my job, but I am fairly certain that I was moved to tears at various points. Time has been kind to me and erased the memory of this experience from my brain. After one season I felt like I'd seen enough. My interest in the show's sixth season, which aired in 2024, was only renewed because I was in a particularly open state of mind and willing to expand my television horizons. In short, I was bored and a little bit sad and needed something to grab me by the eyelashes and drag me out of my ennui.

    I inhaled four episodes in one sitting, transfixed, unable to move from the me-shaped indentation on my sofa. By now *Love Is Blind* has sort of found its stride, and there is a clear-enough playbook for contestants to see what the show can really do for them and their careers. At this point, everyone on the show has a strategy or an idea about what they want and how to get it, whether that's true love or micro-fame within the larger community of Netflix reality show cast members. While Nick and Vanessa still refer to this entire arrangement as an "experiment" in finding true love or whatever, it's clear that this show is just another springboard to fleeting virality or fame. But what made the sixth season so riveting was that almost all the couples that made it through and were engaged to be married were absolutely terrible for each other and even worse at being open and honest about their feelings—and listening to the way they talked about their feelings was a master class in understanding the power of "like," because in every single conversation about big feelings, it was everywhere.

## Megan C. Reynolds

The claustrophobia of the pods gives way to a different sort of claustrophobia once the couples move out and are thrown into the world on their own. When suddenly thrust into close and near-constant contact with another person, you learn a lot. Arguably, some of this information could sway your decisions and thoughts about making a lifelong and very serious commitment to marriage. (I know that it's the point of the show to talk about marriage like it's the ultimate prize, but the way that it is fetishized here made me yell, numerous times, that divorce is an option and we need to acknowledge that!) Essentially, this is the part when things get real—to paraphrase the original entry in the reality TV genre—and everyone loses their shit. Apart from Johnny and Amy, a couple so boring and happy that they don't get a ton of screen time, everyone else is a collective hot mess.

And now the brief ballad of Jimmy and Chelsea, partners who are both toxic in different ways. Attachment theory fetishists would clock the two as stuck in the classic anxious-avoidant trap, where Chelsea chases and Jimmy runs for the hills. They are absolutely horrible together, a gorgeous and sad reality TV train wreck. Whenever these two find themselves drunk and alone, they weaponize their own emotional damage against each other and are seemingly incapable of talking without letting their own shit get in the way. They're not ever direct; they're, like, always trying to figure out why, like, the connection just, like, isn't there?

It becomes clear that both Jimmy and Chelsea know how they feel about each other, and they're doing a horrible job at saying it outright for fear of hurting themselves or the other person. If Chelsea, like, really needs Jimmy to tell her when he's going out and, like, with who and, like, whatever else, what she's really asking for is connection, padding the request out so that it feels smaller and easier to say. This didn't do much for either one of these people in the long run except drive them apart, which was for the best. But even though they weren't meant to get married, they still fancied each other enough to try to be gentle, even as they worked through their own confusion in real time.

When you fill your speech with "like," it facilitates comfort as a hedge, and if you don't think it's doing much of anything except filling the silence, then you're ignoring a useful tool that's sitting right in front of your nose. And even though it sounds like such a minuscule, tiny little thing, "like" is gesturing at something far larger than the sum of its parts: a tiny bid for information and for connection. It's this ineffable human ability to read a room that the robots will never be able to achieve—a breakup text, or a marriage proposal, or some blockbuster superhero psychodrama written by artificial intelligence will always lack a shred of humanity. What makes human connection and conversation truly sound and feel human are the words that we don't think we need (but really do, very much, more than we can say).

■ ■ ■

## Interlude: But What About Texting?

As anyone who has had the immense privilege and honor of sorting through the nightmare stock on a dating app knows, texting can be an incredibly nuanced and enjoyable way to communicate, or, more likely, it fucking sucks. Any of the very important context you get in a face-to-face conversation is gone—facial expressions, body language, and tone of voice all do a fair amount of heavy lifting in an IRL interaction. Yes, this is why and how negging occasionally works, but please know that it *only* works in person. But this lack of nonverbal cues is exactly why online dating, with its interminable meaningless interactions in chat boxes, is so, so awful. Even if that man you talked to for twenty minutes at a weird wine bar down the street turns out to be the worst person alive, perhaps you were able to intuit this by some nonverbal cues that you'd have otherwise missed online.

The trouble with texting is the thing that makes it so appealing. It's a remarkably low-stakes way to reach out and touch somebody (virtually). Texting is, in my mind, a weird and occasionally uncomfortable mash-up between verbal and written communication. And because of texting's dual nature, the mutual understanding is that the words you type into your phone are what you'd say out loud—and the way that you're saying them is the same, too. Texting as your primary form of communication can be fulfilling, but as I will say until the fires take me, context matters.

In a 2019 op-ed for NBC News, psychotherapist Maggie Mulqueen elucidates the issues with texting, starting with the emotional impact, which is by far the most important part of human connection. "The problems with texting begin with the way it reduces conversation to words or photos on a screen; the way it converts the interchange of human connection to brief, stilted fragments," she writes. "That people are in touch through texting with greater frequency and immediacy than ever before means that, ironically, the opportunity for disappointment is also greater."

You don't say.

Texting conflates frequency with good or healthy communication. The very act itself makes a wide berth for allowing all sorts of bad things to filter in, including miscommunications, passive-aggression on a scale much more devastating than in person, and, worst of all, a ton of room for misunderstanding or misinterpretation. Another hellish aspect of the modern condition is that a text exchange can be studied with Talmudic intensity, seeking meaning that would probably not be hidden if you were to hear the same sentence uttered out loud. There is no getting around this kind of thing, anyway. In inconsiderate hands, a text exchange is just a monologue interrupted by someone else's monologue, with none of the natural give-and-take that happens in real life.

Teenagers, bless their hearts, text. A study about the texting habits of teenagers through their adolescence notes that for these young poppets, whose brains are soft, texting is an extremely easy way to experiment with the kind of self-expression that they'd rather keep hidden from their parents. Texting can imitate the cadence of a spoken conversation, but the added benefit, according to the study's authors, is that it's not that weird to take a little time to think before you text—and the medium inherently provides this opportunity.

The easiest way to see if this is true is also the most narcissistic; I am not laboring under the impression that I am extraordinarily interesting, but I do tend toward the anxious in emotionally fraught exchanges, and I must assume this comes out in the way I text. Maybe it's this: Because I worry about almost everything that's out of my control and am also not the best at vulnerability, I try to imbue my texts with the same sort of manic energy I think I convey in public, depending, of course, on the audience. And part of this effort includes typing "like," like, all the time, to mimic the devil-may-care, isn't-she-fun attitude that matches the version of myself that lives in my head.

Poring through your own casual missives is a great exercise in humiliation, but for the sake of this book and for my unfortunate tendency toward analysis in situations that don't require it, I took a look to see what was up. It will not surprise you to hear that reading back your own text messages will really make you think. For example: I "lmao" much more than I "lol." And, yes, I type a lot of "likes" that don't need to be there, precisely because I am trying to convey insouciance. And in these many messages in texts or, embarrassingly, a Slack channel I use primarily to communicate with people I used to work with, I'm typing like I talk, and the result reads manic more so than anything else. This, of course, is a subconscious gesture toward authenticity—I am who I am, and the version of me you get over text, over email, over Slack, or over one glass of wine in person is the same. And if it's, like, pretty important to me that I sound, like, roughly the same here on the page or in a text as I do out there, like, in the real world, where things like bras and hard pants are necessary, then I see no real reason to change my ways.

■ ■ ■

## Interlude: Brass Tacks (Dictionaries)

If you ever find yourself stuck in a library out of necessity rather than intent, a nice way to kill fifteen minutes is to sit down with a dictionary. Yes, the phone you idly tap on and swipe through every minute of the day *also* has a dictionary, and, sure, you could do whatever I'm about to suggest on your phone in two seconds, but stick with me. What the dictionary offers that your dumb little phone doesn't is a sense of discovery. Maybe you harbor suspicions that the idiot you went on a date with two days ago who kept using "limn" as a verb was using it incorrectly. And because this has been bothering you almost nonstop ever since, even though you have no intention of seeing this person again, you are consumed with the desire to prove him wrong.

So off to the dictionary you go, and lo he's right—it is technically correct to say that his half-written novel limns the despair of its protagonist's rich inner life as he grapples with heterosexuality and a looming midlife crisis. According to *Webster's New*

# Like

*World College Dictionary, Fifth Edition*, "limn" is an acceptable verb for the act of description. And while there's nothing specifically in this dictionary or any other that says that this is an irrefutably pretentious way to describe a half-written novel that's trying to do Philip Roth but worse, it's *implied*—this man is a bore, and your ick is valid.

Hear me out: If you often find yourself in situations where you need to prove that what you're saying is correct (or, ideally, that what they're saying is wrong), then being definitionally right matters. And while debating the meanings of words is a fun thing to do at cocktail parties, dictionaries exist for a reason—they're a set of agreed-upon definitions for words and general instructions for how to use them. A dictionary is a living document, always one step behind by the time new editions are published; there's no such thing as a real-time dictionary, because language moves faster than we're able to document. Volumes of the past are like snapshots of those moments in time—useful resources for seeing how far we've come.

There are hundreds, if not thousands, of dictionaries out there, from the most general to the hyperspecific. Urban Dictionary, a long-standing website with user-submitted words and meanings, sets out to define slang written by the audience it's intended for—teenagers. *The Dictionary of Obscure Sorrows*, a Tumblr turned book by John Koenig, is one such dictionary that celebrates the lesser-known words whose meanings are so hyperspecific and romantic in a sense that it'd be difficult to use them in everyday speech. There are dictionaries for English idioms, geared toward English as a Second Language students who have grasped the basics of spoken English but don't understand why someone says that, say, cleaning their gutters is a piece of cake, when the actual activity described is anything but. But the two big boys in the dictionary landscape are arguably *Merriam-Webster* and *Oxford English*, two volumes that work in complement with each other.

The difference between the two is subtle but very important. A 2018 post in the *Columbia Journalism Review* clarifies the distinction: *Merriam-Webster* is synchronic, which means it is a record of how words are used now and focuses on active vocabulary. The *OED* is diachronic, which means it's historical. Both dictionaries are updated and evolve, but *Merriam-Webster* refreshes more frequently as it scrambles to keep pace with the breakneck speed language moves at today. Put it this way: If a word's meaning changes significantly because of, I don't know, a TikTok, the slang definition of that word will show up in *Merriam-Webster* before it does in the *OED*.

"Like" in its slang usage shows up in the fifth edition of *Merriam-Webster*'s doorstopper—a heartening bit of news if you care about language or, frankly, even if you don't. "It's, like, hot" is the example provided, a sentence that I hear in my head and one that I say out loud quite often, maybe too much, but usually as the opening line to my colleagues as we stare at each other in silence before meetings start. How validating! "Inserted into spoken sentences before or after a word, phrase, or clause, apparently without meaning or syntactic function, but possibly for emphasis" is how *Merriam-Webster* says "like" is defined in the slang, and what's beautiful about this definition is the potential for more. "Possibly for emphasis" leaves some room for interpretation, for growth: Right now we're used to people throwing in a "like" when they deem it necessary, but who knows what the future holds?

Dictionaries are about precision, and even though most of the general public thinks that dictionaries are infallible or some sort of final word, let's think about who makes that dusty volume of *Merriam-Webster*. In her book *Word by Word: The Secret Life of Dictionaries*, former *Merriam-Webster* associate editor Kory Stamper provides an engaging and comprehensive account of the Sisyphean task of assembling a dictionary. "A dictionary is out of date the minute that it's done," she writes.

There are only two hard and fast requirements for a hopeful dictionary editor, Stamper writes, and they are relatively minor: Any native English speaker with a degree from a four-year university can apply. And because the dictionary is written by people with different life experiences and backgrounds, part of the training process involves learning how to set aside personal prejudices in the name of pure objectivity. When us normies think about words and, more irritatingly, grammar as "good" or "bad" or "correct," all we're really doing is thinking about the twisting and occasionally arcane rules that we've all been taught that maybe make us feel bad.

Grammar generally creates and disobeys its own rules, then rewrites them, only to do it all over again. This sort of grace and flexibility is because of how these rules came about in the first place: They're just the preferences of the people who were allowed to write the dictionaries of the past, and for some demented reason, we've all sat back and collectively agreed that this is a totally fine way to live. In other words, a dictionary is not prescriptivist, as so many grammarians and general sticks in the muds often are; it's a descriptivist document. "A lexicographer's job is to tell the truth about how language is used," Stamper writes. Lexicographers and linguists share the same impulses—to know as much as they can about language and to help categorize but also facilitate its evolution. "Like" as an entry in the dictionary in all its forms essentially signals mainstream acceptance, and signals to the young lexicographers of the future to make space for the possibility of change.

## Chapter 4

# I Have, Like, One Zillion Things to Do

When I was a sophomore in high school, I moved from the East Coast to the Bay Area to live with my mother. I soon discovered a few very important things: First, there were other half-Asian people in this world—crucially, I wasn't related to them—and, second, everyone around me talked crazy and was very, weirdly cool.

Prior to my journey west, I'd never paid close attention to how I talked or the slang I used, because it wasn't any different from my peers; they were my only frame of reference. Rhinebeck, where I spent most of my formative years, is a town far enough away from the city that specific sayings and slang never naturally ventured that far up the Hudson. (In the winter, it was always just "cold" and never "brick.") Our only excursions into the city were heavily monitored by an adult, so even if we'd managed to escape to try to find Yellow Rat Bastard or the cast of Harmony Korine's *Kids*, I feel certain that we would have been wrangled right back to Grand Central, thrown onto the Metro-North, and sent back up the river to home. There's nothing about Rhinebeck that's particularly edgy, and the town

# Like

I grew up in in the late nineties was not quite as full of expats from Manhattan and surrounding environs as it is today, some five years after the pandemic sent a large chunk of Brooklyn up the Hudson in search of more space, charm, and whatever else. Maybe now, growing up in Rhinebeck conveys something akin to cool—a specific kind meant to be legible to only the young— and if this is the case, I salute those brave foot soldiers. But for myself, I'd be hard-pressed to say that there was anything cool about me at fourteen. After all, I was a product of my environment, and that environment was my house with my father and younger sister and an awful lot of books. And the town itself was claustrophobic enough for me to understand that it was time for me to go.

One of the only real benefits of my parents' divorce was the fact that my mother, stepfather, and two younger sisters lived in California, and because of the custody arrangement, I got to spend every summer there for the majority of my childhood. The story I tell as to why I moved is close enough to the truth that I will share it here: I hated my English teacher, and I wanted to live somewhere with a touch more diversity, and also, as my father reminds me every time my departure comes up, I wanted to see what it was like to live with my mother. The results of this experiment are only to be discussed when all the key players have shuffled off this mortal coil. But this move and the little life I made as a terrifically awkward fourteen-year-old girl, with the confidence but not the bone structure to cut my hair into a pixie cut modeled after Angelina Jolie's in *Hackers*, are now a foundational part of my experience.

**Megan C. Reynolds**

El Cerrito High School was far more diverse than the high school I'd left behind and much bigger—so much so that the arrival of a new student at the beginning of a school year wasn't really cause for commotion. (When my family and I moved to Rhinebeck, I was eight years old and knew just one person—my godmother's daughter, Mali, who, blessedly, having moved to Rhinebeck a year before I did, implicitly understood how important it was to enter this scene with at least one friend. Further context: Two of my oldest friends, both of whom I've known since I was eight, knew each other already from preschool.) Miraculously, I made friends, despite the aforementioned haircut and the vintage Care Bears lunch box I used as a purse. And these friends were all cool in a way that I was not—partly because they were literally quite different from the friends I'd had at home (of the three girls I grew the closest to in high school, Amy was the minority, and, yes, she's white) and also because of the way they spoke. My provincial upbringing was evinced by the way I carried myself; I'm not saying I was a hayseed, but I was not cool. And one word that these people said *did* sound kind of cool, even when it also sounded a little bit stupid.

"Hella" and its more chaste relative, "hecka," are two of Northern California's most enduring legacies, sitting somewhere on the ladder of importance between the rapper E-40 and Apple Inc. Unlike Apple, which is the Bay Area's most valuable cultural export, "hella" is endemic to the Bay. It rarely leaves the borders of Northern California, an easy way to convey where you're from and where you're definitely not from. "Hella" is an intensifier—a word that adds extra oomph and meaning to what follows. Intensifiers are versatile tools that allow for emotional expression in what we're saying. Think about it this way: We use language to describe and summarize emotions and feelings, but intensifiers like "literally," "hella," and "like" allow us to access greater stores of emotional wisdom.

Once I became accustomed to this new manner of speaking, tentatively sprinkling in a "hella" here and there, testing the waters to see if this new, relaxed personality was a fit, I was unstoppable. I don't quite remember the moment when the word clicked for me, but I do know this: Carrying that word back to the East Coast during the summers was my own way of signaling difference and, ideally, a new sort of cool to my friends. "It's hella boring here," I'd say as I flopped onto the sofa at my father's house, exhausted from ennui. I was—and remain—hella dramatic.

We pay extra attention to these intensifiers when they occur in speech because their appearances are rare—words strictly reserved for special occasions, like Aunt Margarita's bone china. Of course, these words don't exist in a vacuum, and the changing nature of language means that some of the words we use today got their start in this very fashion. "Very" is an intensifier that took the place of "really," but if someone says they are really tired, you probably won't blink an eye. And please know that I was shocked—truly—to learn that "very" is bad. Benjamin Dreyer, author of the delightful eponymous style guide *Dreyer's English: An Utterly Correct Guide to Clarity and Style*, calls "very" a "Wan Intensifier" and suggests that you cut the word from your written communication for the sake of clarity. (He allows that it's fine to keep in speech.) Both words are used so frequently now that we don't even bother to think about it—but the beauty of an intensifier is that it allows the speaker to convey a part of their emotional experience in an elegant way. It's a shorthand that speaks volumes, and without it, conversations would suffer.

The use of intensifiers is associated with speech that's emotional rather than descriptive. An example:

> "I really hate cooked carrots."
> "I don't like cooked carrots."

These are two sentences that look very similar but diverge in meaning. The force of your dislike for cooked carrots is present and accounted for in the first; it's not enough to just dislike cooked carrots, because you'd like to take a stance. You don't just hate cooked carrots; you *really* hate them, and you'd like to leave no room for further discussion around the matter. Honestly, I'm intrigued and therefore encouraged to inquire further. But hearing that you don't like cooked carrots? Well, that's a preference and not an absolute, and it leaves just enough room to test some boundaries. You'll have to pick them out of the shepherd's pie, but they'll be in big-enough chunks, so it'll be no work at all. Even though stridently declaring your hatred for a root vegetable sounds extremely dramatic, that's part of the plan. You made a bit of a stink—you pointed to what was important and how you felt about it, while saying very little at all.

One of the greatest strengths of "hella" is how it works to

quantify the physical, but at its essence, it is a classic intensifier, existing to help the speaker really throw their weight behind what's important. You can have hella errands to run, think someone is hella cute or, more often, hella rude. In any of these sentences, if you swap out "hella" for a grammatically correct intensifier, like "so many" or "really," the meaning feels no different. But when you have hella shrimp or there are hella cops, things start to get a little more interesting. As an approximation, "hella" is oriented toward vague exaggeration. "Hella shrimp" is anywhere from one hundred pounds down to at least five, but in this case, precision is not the speaker's intent. The point of the story isn't about how many shrimp there are; it's about how the shrimp made you feel—burdened, inconvenienced, confused.

When used as an intensifier for quantity, "hella" has a tidy elegance that other words lack. Here are three sentences describing the same scene:

"There are so many horses running down the beach right now!"

"There are hella horses running down the beach right now!"

"There are, like, one thousand horses running down the beach right now!"

These sentences are all conveying the same physical information—there's a beach, there are horses, they're running down the beach. But the way this information is conveyed and the one little change used to convey it demonstrate how vital intensifiers are to feeling understood. If I hear you say there are so many horses running down the beach, I'm hearing a sense of wonder at the beauty of the world. The presence of these horses cantering in the sun's early rays is a memory that you will call upon whenever your general faith in humanity wavers. Also—and maybe more importantly—I assume that you knew the horses were coming or were pleasantly surprised by this experience; in short, their presence is not distressing, and their numbers are not so big as to be life-threatening. I'm thinking, like, ten horses, tops. In short, a beautiful *Misty of Chincoteague* moment that leaves you invigorated and also at ease.

"Hella horses," on the other hand, is another thing entirely. "Hella horses" frankly sounds like too many horses, and the precise number isn't important to me or the story at this time. This is a serious matter; there is danger and distress. No one told you there'd be horses, because they knew you wouldn't have come; this is a trick that's impolite and to be discussed further at dinner, but for now, here you are, pinned flat against a sand dune, watching too many goddamn horses sprint down the beach as your anxiety rises. Some questions remain: Where did the horses come from? Why are they there? Also, why are you? Can you leave? Are you okay? "Hella horses" are one step above a stampede, and the exact number doesn't matter, because that bit needs no further explanation: It's simply too many. It is too much.

"Like" and "hella" both do the same thing but in different ways—"like" relies on specificity and "hella" obscures the details. The *Oxford English Dictionary* notes that "hella" is a special kind of adverb that can modify basically anything. It is shockingly difficult to find any real academic work on the place of "hella" in speech, but perhaps that's because the generation of linguists who would be concerned with this sort of thing is still on the come up. A senior thesis written by Peter Le, then a student at the University of California, Davis, is a comprehensive introductory view into the use of "hella." "Speakers use 'hella' as an intensifier modifying a variety of lexical categories, including verbs, adjectives, and adverbs," he writes. "'Hella' acts as a universal intensifier for adjectives, adverbs, and verbs, assuming the roles of both 'very' and 'really.'" We understand, then, that if "hella" is in front of any of those kinds of words, the point that you're trying to make is potentially hyperbolic, but not so much so that you'd be outright lying.

But what "like" and "hella" both do in casual conversations about serious things is convey emotional nuance or, at the very least, display any emotion at all. They let you understand the emotional impact of what's being said. And our speech and communication would be dull without both. What's the fun in a conversation between friends that lacks exaggeration for dramatic effect? In my opinion as well as in practice, I think both "hella" and "like" can be an invitation to a challenge. If I said there were hella pigeons at the beach (or, like, 975) that one time, and you, also present at the beach that day, disagree, I can't imagine the disagreement is rooted in real anger. We're engaging in healthy debate. We're doing a bit. Lighthearted. Not serious. Imprecision can be useful in conversations between friends, especially when the focus is less on the facts and more on the feelings.

As parts of speech, both "like" and "hella" are discourse

markers and are therefore grammatically optional—they don't change the true meaning of a sentence and so are technically extraneous bits of chatter crammed into our sentences. But what discourse markers do as a part of speech is utilitarian in nature: They provide "nuanced pragmatic information" that helps a conversation move smoothly along, according to a study of discourse markers' use among autistic children. "Some see discourse markers as empty, fulfilling no semantic role. According to this interpretation, the appropriate meaning of [discourse markers] depends on their surrounding context, and the marker itself does not add any meaning; therefore it can be deleted from a text without any apparent sacrifice to meaning," the study reads.

Definitionally, they're useless—if they don't significantly alter the meaning of a sentence, one might argue, then what's the point? That's a stinky attitude that's also wrongheaded and ignores another crucial facet of interpersonal communication: nuance, which is precisely what that statement lacks. "Like" does work as an approximation in a way that's easy to see, but what's even more interesting is when it does double duty and pulls focus to that which it is approximating. In a 2003 study written by Janet M. Fuller, a sociolinguist at Southern Illinois University in Carbondale, about the use of the word in interviews, she gestures at how this application of the word allows for more specificity. "The overlap of these two functions makes sense; there is no reason to indicate approximation of something that is not important in the sentence, and conversely, if something is the focus of the sentence, you want to make sure that, if approximate, this looseness of meaning is marked," she writes. An example will perhaps clarify once more: Let's rewind to the story of too many horses on the beach.

"There are, like, one thousand horses running down the beach right now!" is a statement where "like" allows for nuance. As the person experiencing this equine situation, I am less concerned with the specifics and would like to direct my audience toward the thing that matters; in this case, it's the sheer number of horses that were unexpectedly galloping down this beach and, more importantly, that I felt overwhelmed by the situation because of how many horses there were. Too many to count in my panicked state, but way more than is necessary or welcome.

Though often I feel it would be much easier if the world were black-and-white, I've finally come around to the idea of the gray area—the nightmarish liminal space where paradox lives and everyone understands the fundamental concept that two things can be true at once. Many things flourish in this rich landscape, including mutual understanding, vulnerability, connection, and joy. And it's those feelings, most of which are positive or only uncomfortable for a little bit, where intensifiers do some very important work.

I suppose there's some value in prioritizing efficiency in speech, but these discourse markers are efficient in their own way: emotional efficiency, which is something I just made up. Emotions are inherently inefficient because they are feelings, not facts, and you never really know how they're going to move. And "hella" and "like" make it so that you don't have to be explicit and say, "Hey, buddy, this is how I feel, and I'm not afraid to say it." They're tiny flares instead, directing your audience to the thing that's really important—the heart of what you're trying to say. It's an act of kindness for you that also serves your audience by gently urging them to keep the fuck up.

There is no argument that the quotative use of "like" is by far the most reviled. But I'm sure you're shocked to learn that this function of the word is despised almost as much. It will also shock you to hear that this usage is largely associated with young women. Regardless of how the particular "like" is actually functioning in a sentence, this is the one they wish to kill through public speaking courses; shame-y, priggish op-eds; software designed to remove it from audio; and various apps for your little telephone that promise to make you sound "articulate," as if the way you normally speak is something to be corrected.

Speeko is one such app, touted as being a personal speech coach in your pocket and uses, naturally, the power of AI. The app will analyze your speech for filler words, tone, sentiment, and other metrics in an attempt to provide you with a full and well-rounded portrait of just how dumb you sound when you speak in professional settings and what, if anything, can be done about it. The idea of being better-spoken is intriguing. I'm articulate. I think about my words probably a little too much before I say them, as if the right phrase can control an outcome that's completely out of my hands. And, crucially, I don't have any desire to shift my professional personality to sound like anything other than myself. Clearly, I am not the target audience. But natural curiosity and a sense of duty drew me to Speeko, where, for an afternoon, I tried to see if my phone could help me sound like more of an adult.

According to the charming intro video, spark, body, breath, and voice are the four components of your own personal voice. Mastering a command of all four will make your spoken communication sound intentional, powerful, persuasive—strong enough to command the attention of an entire boardroom full of half-drunk CEOs and keep it for the duration of your thirty-six-slide deck. This argument was compelling enough to keep me engaged, but when it came time to engage in movement warm-ups that felt vaguely like embarrassing theater games, I was about ready to tap out. About ten minutes into my experience with Speeko, I wondered if the app was gaslighting me. When starting a lesson about filler words and how to get rid of them, I noticed that the app's definition of "eloquence" and my personal definition (and understanding) differed slightly. "In the setting of public speaking, the fewer filler words you use, the more well-spoken and confident you sound," Speeko tells me. "We call this area of vocal delivery 'eloquence.'"

My understanding of eloquence has little to do with filler words or, really, the words that are spoken at all, but with the overall impression you leave when you're done speaking. Eloquent speech is gently persuasive, it is fluent, it is never strident—the kind of speech that is a little bit beautiful, which endears it to and impacts its intended audience. Speeko is in part designed to teach confidence, so one presumes that filler words, of any sort, in any situation, are eroding your audience's ability to take you seriously. If you buy into this wholesale, you will start paying closer attention to the way that you talk, and instead of celebrating it for whatever it is because you're a special snowflake (sincerely!), you will start to give yourself demerits for every "like," "um," "uh," "actually," and "so." You will mentally start to track your speech in real time while assessing how cluttered it is with garbage. And then, once you've gotten any zip of personality out of your speech, you are ready to conquer the world.

Words like "eloquent" and "articulate," both used when we talk about proper and persuasive speech, are especially charged when they come to speakers of color. Despite the racist undertones of these words when deployed with cruelty, being articulate or eloquent has nothing to do with race. One imagines that other apps and programs designed like Speeko don't set out with the intention to teach how to speak like white people. Ideally—and in practice—all these apps are doing is parroting the same dusty notions of what sounds "right" and calling it eloquence.

But if we turn to the dictionary, we'll see that the general definition of eloquence includes persuasion as a metric. I'd argue that there are situations in which intensifiers like "hella" and "like" are extraordinarily persuasive. If you know there are, like, a thousand cops by that speed trap, and you heard this from someone you trust, I'd reckon that you don't need to know how many cops there actually are—you'll take the long way home. If I were to look out my back window and see hella people milling about the usually empty and questionably legal weed deli down the block, and then recount this story saying, specifically, that there were hella people at the weed deli, everyone listening would be on the same page. It doesn't matter how many people there actually were—it's clear that there was a remarkable amount, we don't know why they're all there, and this is maybe good news for the weed deli employees and also for Mimi, the store cat. The sentence functions fine without "hella," but when it's missing, we are left with no road map to the speaker's emotional state and therefore have no solid information about how to modulate our own in response. What "like" and "hella" do is important to good speech—they provide the spark that ignites meaningful conversation.

All the people up in arms about teenage girls sounding, like, completely stupid for saying "like," like, all the time are missing the point. Of course there's value in being direct, but it's not always necessary. "Like" allows you to point at what you need or how you feel without screaming that you need it, and this small act of kindness allows you a modicum of control over your unruly emotions without having to tamp them down entirely. As "hella" serves as shorthand for abundance and overwhelm, "like" is just as pliant. It pulls focus, draws you in, and points at what's actually important: how something makes you feel.

To illustrate this point, I present some flash fiction about a marriage on the rocks:

*"I don't know where Alfredo's lederhosen are, Elizabeth, and I can't, like, stop everything I'm doing, like, right now to look for them, because the cat's, like, screaming for dinner and I've had to*

*pee for, like, twelve hours."* Andrea sighed. *She put down the dish towel. She turned swiftly on her heel and walked into the powder room, never to be seen again.*

Let's unpack this rich text. Alfredo's lederhosen are missing, which is important—but not as important as Andrea's emotional state and stress levels, both of which seem elevated. Andrea could really use some help finding the German trousers, but the cat's sustenance and, most importantly, that she's had to pee for half of a calendar day take precedence. If push came to shove, I'd say all these problems carry equal weight and all of them are indeed real problems. Andrea is pressed for bandwidth. The tiny pile of tasks that populate these days is starting to feel burdensome. They need childcare so that Alfredo's lederhosen are never lost and he never feels shame at day care. And clearly, Andrea and Elizabeth need to sit down together to figure out why both the cat and their son are catching the strays from their conflict.

Most of what I've taken from that bad but honest attempt at fiction is just inference. Nothing about my conclusions is rooted in any explicitly stated truth, but the likes are the signposts that led my way to the important stuff. When used in this way, "like" does gentle emotional labor, allowing you a hint of distance from a big feeling. And just as its presence signals that there's more information to be had, its absence shares all the information you need.

There's a brief moment in the opening number of Disney's 1991 *Beauty and the Beast* that illustrates this point. As the sun rises on the provincial town Belle lives in, she sings a rousing song processing her complicated feelings about her hometown—relatable! She loves it, she knows it, she hates it, she wants more. On this musical journey, we meet just about everyone, from the baker to the butcher to the little gnome man who runs the bookstore. But the brightest star in this universe is a housewife jostling three infants in her arms, with two more children grabbing at her skirts. She thrusts a basket into the face of a confused man, whom I assume is the egg vendor at the local farmer's market. "I! Need! Six Eggs!" she shrieks, the desperation in her voice rising to a fever pitch. Alas, we will never know her fate because Belle, swinging off the back of a wagon, drives the plot along and away from this tragic scene.

Unfortunately, to really understand the impact of this scene, it's necessary to watch it—but even if you don't, I think this woman's hysterical, harried, and iconic countenance comes through. There is no denying the urgency of this situation. Notice how there is no hesitation in this woman's assertion; she needs the eggs. She needs six of them, no more, no less, and she's so stressed out that she actually doesn't have the energy to hear out the price at this bougie farmer's market. There is nothing casual about the situation, and there is no room for questions. She needs the eggs. Please get her the eggs.

If we add a "like," the entire scenario changes. "I need, like, six eggs," even if delivered with the same sense of urgency, is not really the same thing at all. Is it just six eggs? Is it maybe three? Is it actually just one egg, but you're so stressed out that asking for anything more than the bare minimum is too much for you to handle, and, really, maybe you're asking for six, but you definitely need fifteen? These are all valid questions that beg for answers and are raised by the "like" sidling in. And, arguably, these are more interesting questions I'd ask than in the original scene, where this woman is assertive about her needs and then dismissive of them immediately after. That tells me all I need to know—but in this scenario, my attention is called to the eggs and, more importantly, what her desire for the eggs represents. I'm being asked to pay attention, to see that there's something below the surface, and to find out why.

This is a singular example, to say the least; it is clear that the urgency of this woman's message is diluted if she approximates the number of eggs she's howling about, but this does prove a point. When you approximate a detail that would otherwise feel important, the implication is that the precise facts don't matter. "Like" facilitates conversations because it allows for exaggeration, for hyperbole, and for fun. It's casual, conspiratorial, and familiar; without it sprinkled here and there, our conversations would lose their zest. Precision does have its place, even in friendships, where part of the whole deal is that, if it's a good one, the communication can be almost nonverbal. But a friendship is not a meeting with Human Resources or a police interrogation, two situations in which precision seems paramount. If my friend tells me they need, like, six frozen margaritas and five cigarettes at the end of a long week, I don't need to press on the specifics—what's implied is just enough.

■ ■ ■

## Interlude: Why Is It Women?

While there are reams of research that support the assertion that young women are the innovators of linguistic change, in order for me—and, ostensibly, you—to really believe this information, we should take a closer look at how this assertion came to be. William Labov, a linguistics professor at the University of Pennsylvania, pioneered the research that led to this fact, which is instrumental in understanding why people get upset with teenage girls for the way they talk—and why, despite these people's ire, they end up sounding like teenage girls anyway.

In his 1990 paper "The intersection of sex and social class in the course of linguistic change," Labov observes two contradictions. Men generally use more "nonstandard" forms of words than women, especially in "stable sociolinguistic stratification," which is just academic jargon for words that mean different things in the same social setting. But when it comes to actual linguistic change—new ways of using words, thereby

115

changing their meaning—women generally use more nonstandard forms than men. One reason for this contradiction is that men are perhaps using nonstandard forms because there's little to no social stigma attached to the way they speak—so if a man uses improper grammar or is slangier when he speaks, we're less apt to notice it because, I'm sorry, he's a man. Women, on the other hand, hew close to the standards, minding their p's and q's, precisely because of the inherent social stigma attached to their speech patterns and vocabulary.

Frustratingly, none of this feels very codified or written in stone. "Either sex can be the dominant factor," Labov writes of linguistic change. "But the number of cases where men are in the lead is relatively small." The changes led by men don't leave much of a mark and are therefore less impactful than the changes led by women. While men may be faster in glomming on to change that feels significant, women are actually doing the work of making the change stick.

Penelope Eckert, a linguistics professor at Stanford University, writes that, traditionally, women are the caretakers, and so our first real exposure to how a person should sound and act is exemplified by our mothers. (There are lots of people, myself included, who were raised primarily by men. While I cannot speak for anyone else, I don't think that my father's child-rearing method, which I once categorized in a college admissions essay as "benign neglect," negatively impacted the development of my speech patterns, nor has it held me back in any significant way.) As you grow and start to form your own identity, you undergo a phase of "vernacular reorganization"—

what happens when the way you learned how to speak via your mother or otherwise becomes different and starts to change. The vernacular of your childhood switches to the vernacular of your adolescence, as you find your own identity by speaking like your friends, social media influencers, or whomever else you're exposed to, as a means of setting yourself apart from your parents and finding your own path.

As girls grow up and find their way in the world, the ambient sense of powerlessness that often plagues children becomes more acute.

"Whether or not they wielded any direct power in their childhoods, adolescent girls know full well that their only hope is through personal authority," Eckert writes. For her purposes as well as our own, "authority" really means social capital and popularity—the shiny prize that they can eventually buy. Though this will sound both rude and like a stereotype, the science backs it up: Girls are routinely more concerned with seeking out popularity than boys are, because girls understand that they need this powerful tool in order to achieve a modicum of high school success. Granted, Eckert's information is taken from her book *Jocks and Burnouts: Social Categories and Identity in the High School*, a study of the population of a Detroit-area high school in the early 1990s. The desire for popularity is not limited strictly by gender; boys also seek popularity as well as acceptance, but they go about it in different ways.

Boys gain access to status and power through physical prowess and "direct action"—a polite way of saying that teenage boys are reduced to their basest and most cavemen-like instincts, using their burgeoning physical strength to assert dominance. A star football player, of the sort valorized in small towns and television shows like *Friday Night Lights*, is the king of his very specific domain, based solely on his athletic skills. Other factors, like physical attractiveness and intelligence, are less of a consideration, because if you can make a sixty-four-yard touchdown from the line of scrimmage, then what else really matters? Boys are allowed to use their accomplishments as a form of power and social capital, whereas girls of the same age have to be, as Eckert writes, "a certain sort of person."

A paper published in 2009 by Alexandra D'Arcy and Sali A. Tagliamonte corroborates the notion that the most significant language changes occur in adolescence, and those changes are largely led by women. But just because women *are* the leaders in linguistic change doesn't mean that men don't make some changes of their own—and it also doesn't mean that men necessarily follow suit. In fact, thanks to the theory of gender asymmetry, the research suggests that once a way of speaking becomes associated with women, due in part to the fact that women are the ones who started saying the new thing in the new way, men clock it as inherently negative and run screaming for the hills.

Nothing about this explanation feels definitive—just theories backed up by data, and, as I have learned, half the gag of academia is spending a lot of energy assessing, analyzing, and occasionally refuting the work of your colleagues by beefing in academic journals that maybe twenty people read. The answer to the central question of "why is it women" is standard misogyny—even if you, as a woman, don't feel like you're being sidelined by the men around you, I'd bet five dollars and one doughnut that you have been at some point in your life, just because you are a woman.

## Chapter 5

# Like, It's Sexist?

Allow me for a moment to return to the Sherman Oaks Galleria and revisit the Valley Girl who's sitting in the food court, drinking an Orange Julius. In 1982, at the height of Valley Girl–mania, a speech pathologist named Dr. Lillian Glass published *How to Deprogram Your Valley Girl*, a manual-cum-field-guide for confused parents wanting to change their daughters' speech before the terrible habits they incurred in adolescence calcified in adulthood. "The exercises in this book can give you the confidence to become the best speaker, whether you are talking to one person or a room of thousands," the description reads. What a relief.

Cracking the spine on Glass's classic reveals nothing terrifically revelatory—in under one hundred pages, the book covers basic principles of good public speaking habits, from breath control to rhythm and pacing—but it's aimed at a very specific audience: parents of the early eighties who were genuinely befuddled by the alien creature that replaced their precious baby girl and who were desperate for a solution.

Glass provides an overview in the briefest of terms on how

powerful Southern California's impact was on the culture. Because Valley Girls were born out of the excess of the eighties, the culture was naturally capitalistic—the young denizens of the Valley responsible for bringing about this change were mostly concerned with buying stuff at the mall. "Most conversation, in fact, revolves around things: who has what, whose is better," writes Glass.

The book opens as a guide book of sorts, meant to illustrate the life cycle of a Valley Girl, from inception in tweenhood to its eventual end. This path is just a stylized description of the onset of adolescence, though it is worth noting that from the look of things, the tweens of today would have likely eaten the teens of 1982 for breakfast. In her pupal form, a Valley Girl is just a regular girl, unsullied by the outside pressures of conformity and acceptance. Her clothing is functional, she wears little makeup, she speaks "American English," and she would make an excellent Girl Scout—in short, a girl who is acceptable by society's standards and therefore will sail through her life unhindered, not because she stands out but because she blends in. The transformation to Valley Girl starts with clothing and appearance, as the plain jeans and tees of tweendom transform into makeup, gold jewelry, miniskirts, and shoulder pads. These sartorial changes are not the only sign that worries parents—they offer a curious, clipped manner of speaking and a new vocabulary that signal the true start of the Valley Girl transformation.

Emphasizers like "oh my god" and "totally" pepper sentences, leaving the rest of the words in their surroundings a jumbled and monotonous mess seemingly indecipherable to adult ears. When the process is over, the Valley Girl has emerged as the beautifully tacky butterfly—her final form—much to the chagrin and disappointment of her hapless parents. "Parents and children have now become a complete embarrassment to one another," Glass writes. "They are spared excessive contact by the fact that the full-blown Valley Girl spends at least as much time at the shopping mall as she does at home, and the charge-card bills are a small price to pay for not having her around."

Even though Glass's text is not meant to be taken all that seriously, perhaps it's obvious that sexism is part of the issue here. Yes, the stereotypical image of a Valley Girl, as laid out in the book and in the media of the era, likes shopping, makeup, fashion, and anything else that will ultimately help optimize her appearance for men, sure, but also for herself. But nowhere in the foundational text about Valley Girls does it say anything about their intelligence, though all this criticism is thick with implication—women who care about things like their appearance are naturally less intelligent, because to care this deeply about such a thing is clearly a sign of an empty head. I'm hopeful that in our modern age, I don't have to explain too much about why this is wrongheaded, but just so that my stance on this is clear: You can care about fashion, buying things, and jewelry while also caring about *other*, different things, like the looming threat of world war, the melting polar ice caps, and whatever else people might think is "serious."

In the interest of fairness, Glass dedicates a small section of the book to Valley Dudes, perhaps to ward off any cries of sexism—but this particular specimen gets less than half the real estate dedicated to his female counterpart.

Anyway, once you've effectively determined that a Valley Girl lives among you, it's time to deprogram the "like," "totally," and "for sure" out of her vocabulary, once and for all. Suggestions for this process include cutting off access to credit cards and telephones, and scrubbing the offenders of their makeup and plumage—all jokes, of course, but still viewed in the book as temporary fixes for what could be a permanent issue. Glass says that most people will outgrow this manner of speaking, because as you grow out of your teens and start limping toward adulthood, you realize that the world is bigger than what you know and that you'll have to figure out some other ways of fitting in.

The fear here is that the ways we start speaking as teenagers, when we're in the midst of forming our actual identities and are therefore experimenting with light rebellion, are the ways that we'll speak for the rest of our lives, for better or worse. But, Glass explains, with both time and patience, you can beat these habits out of your kids. Though she is absolutely not advocating corporal punishment, the tools she provides parents would probably feel like it to a teen starting to figure themselves out. Imagine being fourteen years old and being forced to endure public speaking lessons led by your parents—a nightmarish scenario that has a long history in the United States and beyond. The elocution movement of the mid-nineteenth century in the United States advocated for clarity in spoken communication; if you were a teen of a certain social standing, your parents might have sent you out for elocution lessons so that you sounded less like a guttersnipe and more like an upper-class member of society. Breath control and pitch modulation, which are both tactics meant to train the speaker to slow down, to be considerate, and to think holistically before speaking, are all useful tools for, say, a junior senator looking to make an impression, but are overkill for a teen of today just trying out a new identity.

Even though Glass's book—and the arguments contained therein—is largely outdated and over forty years old, the general question about how to fix the inherent wrongness of women's speech is eternal. Just as soon as any public intellectual takes to their pulpit to denounce and criticize those who use filler words, there's inevitably a backlash to the backlash, as others rise to their defense. In 2005 third-wave feminist turned QAnon conspiracy theorist Naomi Wolf, author of *The Beauty Myth: How Images of Beauty Are Used Against Women,* wrote a piece for *The Guardian* warning women against vocal fry and uptalk, while questioning the intelligence of all those whose speech is full of such junk. Her research shows that of all the people who dislike these speech mannerisms, along with the use of filler words like "like," the major critics (besides herself) are older men. "Does cordially hating these speech patterns automatically mean you are anti-feminist?" she posits, and then, for a few more paragraphs, attempts to prove herself wrong. For Wolf, young women relying on vocal fry, filler words, and uptalk as a subtle and polite power grab in conversations is a setback rather than an advantage. Young women have come so far, she argues, so why would they undermine themselves and, by extension, undo the hard-won progress feminists like Wolf and her cohort worked so hard to achieve?

To be clear: It's not really useful to consider anything Naomi Wolf says anymore, if only because she has destroyed any shred of credibility by subscribing wholeheartedly to anti-vax rhetoric and has since been banned from social media and, in a way, public life because of this particular pivot. The criticism of young women and the way they speak is both sexist and retrograde. Wolf's argument isn't necessarily anti-feminist, partly because feminism has many stripes and, as a nightmarish man I dated once told me, it's not just a scarf that you can put on or take off when it's convenient. But if we separate the feminism question from her general argument, I think we can all agree that Naomi Wolf is preaching to a largely empty room.

Even though I'd agree that the majority of the population that needs to concern itself with credibility has already reckoned with its own personal speech demons, the argument against the way women speak persists. In 2017 *The New York Times* published an article about filler words and how to stop using them in everyday conversations. (I'll note that this subject is a particular favorite at the *Times*, perhaps because Columbia linguistics professor John McWhorter has an opinion column where they'll let him rattle on about pretty much anything.) While the article itself was not explicitly sexist, like all the others of its ilk it *was* prescriptive, and we can be realistic in presuming whom the prescriptions were directed toward. Using filler words is actually making you sound stupider, argues Christopher Mele, the author of this article, and instead of shortchanging yourself by speaking in a manner that belies your intelligence, if you trim the fat from your verbal communication, the world will lie at your feet.

Mele's argument is hardly new; for longer than the Valley Girl stock character has existed, there have been people clinging to outdated senses of propriety who refuse to acknowledge the one crucial rule about language: It does not live in a vacuum. Language is a constantly evolving swirling mass, and it necessarily changes, usually for the better, if "better" in this instance means "unlike the dusty ways of the past." And, frankly, the call is coming from inside the house—even if listening to a teenage girl of today speak is a little bit like nails on a chalkboard, chances are that some of their cadences, their words, and their particular turns of phrase are already a part of your speech. You might not even notice the offending phrase, because saying it feels and sounds natural—you'll only start to pay attention when (and if) you face criticism, constructive or otherwise.

When writing a book about a word that people say so much that it's like breathing, I found that when I mentioned it, people were very forthcoming about their use of the word—and, more specifically, monitoring its presence. At least two or three of my friends—whip-smart, self-aware women—said to me that they notice how much they say the word "like" and that they need to stop. When pressed as to why this need feels so urgent, the explanation was vague and slightly self-deprecating, though the gist of it is basically that they think they sound stupid, unsure, and like they're using a crutch to lean on in situations where they should be able to stand on their own two feet. And, not to belabor the point, but this is usually because the terms of what sounds "dumb" or otherwise are generally set by men—a fact that matters to them, of course, but not so much to women. In fact, the way women speak among themselves and in the greater world holds currency with other women and those who respect them, and as I have said to many friends, strangers, and anyone who will listen, the way you talk is not inherently wrong, even if you're a woman and "like" is every other word that comes out of your mouth.

"Like" and its cousin "uptalk" are two nuances of spoken communication that are both largely tied to women and how they speak. For all of feminism's various victories, policing the way women speak and therefore making women feel as if they need to police themselves, even subconsciously, is a sport that will never get old. To say that this is tremendously irritating is an understatement. We should all be embarrassed that this subject is still up for discussion! Life is full of disappointments both large and small, and weathering those indignities is hard enough—dragging language into the fray is unnecessary and, frankly, a bit rude. I look to what my friend Emily refers to as the Bible—2001's *Bridget Jones's Diary*, a movie that, despite being over twenty years old, really holds up. "Every time I see you, you seem to go out of your way to make me feel like a complete idiot," Bridget (Renée Zellweger, in the role of a lifetime, at the peak of her powers) says to the perpetually brooding Mark Darcy (Colin Firth, the OG Mr. Darcy, very hot). "And you really needn't bother: I already feel like an idiot most of the time anyway."

In short, there are enough things to worry about in this one precious life, and I can't speak for everyone, but I can say with confidence that for me, I'm already good at making myself feel bad. And given the state of the world today, beating myself up for how dumb I sound when I tell someone that it's, like, totally fine if they give me that thing I need by, like, hm, the end of next week, is a tremendous waste of my time and energy. Let me decide what I want to be upset at myself for today without throwing any more logs on the fire, thank you!

As a woman, I choose the words I use and how I say them in a way that tends naturally toward accommodation anyway—even if some jerk tells me that my long-windedness and flair for the dramatic are detracting from my credibility, it doesn't matter. First of all, this imaginary person's opinion of the way I speak has nothing to do with my opinion of myself, and second, maybe there's some strategy behind my verbosity and hyperbole—to make other people feel comfortable and to let them know that I'm serious when I need to be, but I default to court jester, so, please, respond in kind. I rarely notice this kind of care or attention paid when speaking to most, but not all, men.

If "like" is the one word that's associated with women's speech and bandied about as the very thing that will end civilization if we let it, one wonders: What about men? We've proven very thoroughly that women are linguistic innovators and that they drive language's changes and evolution forward. And while it'd be nice to sometimes close your eyes and pretend that we live in a world where whatever men are doing doesn't matter, I suppose for this particular exercise, it's useful to see if there are any reasonable comparisons to make. Surely if women are internalizing the belief that saying "like" too much will ruin any chance they have at success or power, men must have a word or phrase that also compromises their position at the top.

To be clear: It's not sexist or anti-feminist to say that men and women speak differently, simply because it's true—it's the direct result of years of socialization toward outdated gender roles with which we are all familiar by now. However, that's not to say that there isn't a male equivalent that's been met with some but not nearly as much criticism as "like."

"Dude"—and its contemporary, "bro" and other variations ("breh," "bruh," etc.)—is a word largely associated with men that serves just as many grammatical uses as "like." It's a greeting, a sign-off, an indication of approval or disapproval, a means of emphasis. And it's a word that's almost as gendered as "like" can be. Just like you might beat yourself up on the inside every time you hear yourself speak out loud when you have to, say, present a slide in a Zoom call about information that you learned ten minutes ago, there are people out there who get mad when a man calls someone "dude" who simply isn't one. But this isn't nearly as big of an offense regardless of how ridiculous it is, and that doesn't really track. An example ripped from the pages of my own life: My youngest sister, Shaina, has a habit of telling our mother, a diminutive powerhouse who is too short to reach the top of the fridge but runs half-marathons and 10ks in her free time, to "calm down, bro." This occurs usually in texts and never fails to make me laugh. What else am I supposed to do? My sister isn't constructing an elaborate argument about why calling our mother "bro" ("dude's" cooler cousin) makes her sound stupid—she's technically latching onto some of the cultural capital "dude" imparts and using the word to convey a casual, detached, and ineffable cool in the face of our mother, a woman who is many things but not stereotypically "cool."

In simpler terms, "dude," "bro," "bruh," and any deviations occupy a lot of the same linguistic space that "like" does. The difference is that generally "dude" can also be described as a vibe, and "like" not so much at all. However, "dude" is a different part of speech than "like," and when used as a verbal crutch, it occupies much of the same expectations about gender that "like" does—and it's an easy bugbear for grammarian snobs to feel upset about, just like with "like." And now, at the risk of inadvertently offending someone, allow me to make two generalizations that will probably rankle but, like these statements so often do, contain a kernel of truth.

Through their speech, women often want to come off as fashionable, aloof, cool, and cutting-edge, which befits their societal role as trendsetters—think of influencers, their speech habits. (If this isn't ringing a bell for you, grab the telephone of a young person, navigate to TikTok, and scroll through their For You page, which will likely make you feel very old but will also make this point clear.) Men, on the other hand, have very different needs: They want to sound like "men"—masculine, strong, powerful, and, yes, in case it wasn't obvious, very heterosexual. And if we peek behind the curtain at the rise of "dude," we can understand a little more how the word is the unlikely analogue to "like."

According to the *Oxford English Dictionary*, "dude" is a Gilded Age artifact used to describe a fancy man—one who cares a lot about his appearance and who could also be described as a "fop" or a "dandy." If it is difficult for you to imagine what a fancy man from the late nineteenth century would even look like, let's use a modern-day example that might make more sense. The fin de siècle dude, with his velvet top hats, satin waistcoats, and fastidious attention to sartorial details, is the great-great-great-grandfather of another particular type of modern man—the design-oriented, fashion-concerned man, generally straight, usually city-dwelling, with a predilection for "menswear," "streetwear," unfortunate hats, and an inability to construct an outfit that conveys any semblance of personality.

This man, the streetwear nightmare, has listened to every single episode of the podcast *Throwing Fits*. He makes interesting choices with his trousers and can often be found scouring the internet for an alternative to the USM Haller media console that he keeps seeing on Instagram (too expected; everyone has one)—something that plays well with his vintage IKEA lighting and preferred chair of note, whether it be an Eames lounge chair or a Wassily. Though they understand and will say in mixed company that Kanye West's pivot from provocateur to full-on wackadoodle makes it impossible to listen to his music, they still think that the Axel Vervoordt–designed home West shared with his ex-wife, Kim Kardashian, is a stroke of subversive design genius, and they'll offer this opinion whether you care or not. In short, were you to find yourself face-to-face with this person on a date, you would start looking for a polite way to leave.

This particular person shares similarities with another kind of "cool" man, the hypebeast, but you would never find a streetwear nightmare lining up for a drop of a sneaker that is ugly but has an aura of cool—technically, these men are two sides of the same "dude" coin. And if we follow this thread to its natural conclusion, the very specific kind of cool that "dude" conveys is embodied by someone who sits squarely in between these two poles: a man secure enough in his masculinity to wear non-Nantucket pastels and outlandish pants—not because other people think it's cool, but because he does, and so it is.

Much like how "like" has taken on a life of its own, the "dude" we know now started out as referring to a very specific concept and has evolved into something completely different. Originally, to call someone a "dude" was a bit of an insult; no one wanted to be called a dude, no matter how well-made their foppy little waistcoat was, but it was an easy way to self-identify. And thanks to language's inherently evolving nature, the meaning of "dude" evolved, referring to men who stood out because of their attire, but it has been stripped of any of the word's previous feminine—and therefore negative—connotations. It was this transit that allowed for the word to travel the road from insult to inoffensive and then to cool. Language change is driven by the counterculture and those who exist on the fringes of society. In "You've Come a Long Way, Dude: A History," Richard

Hill notes that "dude" only gained a sheen of cool when "urban Mexican American pachucos and African American zoot-suiters began referring to themselves as dudes." And the way "dude" entered the popular slang lexicon is a tale as old as time: White men, desperate for a soupçon of that cachet, started using it, too. After enough time, the word's definition moved away from referring to clothing and instead became a catch-all term for just a guy—not necessarily a regular guy but a cool-enough one. You know, like, a dude.

Scott Kiesling, professor in the Department of Linguistics at the University of Pittsburgh, is the author of the most definitive study I've found on "dude." In a paper published in *American Speech* in 2004, Kiesling argues that "dude" is portraying both men's solidarity with their fellow men but also a specifically heterosexual image of masculinity. Men call one another "dude" so that the other men in their cohort don't think they're gay. And the solidarity that "dude" cultivates is a level of bonding that men only allow themselves to experience when bound together in service, like in the military or a fraternity—two institutions that were built on strong foundations of traditional manly shit. Dude both repels and attracts: It assures other men that there's a level of understanding, but under no circumstances are these feelings romantic or sexual in nature.

Kiesling's study comes from a corpus of observations at a fraternity at the University of Pittsburgh in 1993 and college classrooms at the same school a decade later. In studying these populations, Kiesling found that "dude" routinely appears at the opening or the closing of a sentence or a statement—equal parts invocation and conclusion. And much like "like" has evolved to embody different parts of speech, so has "dude." A "dude" disarms possible conflict and is also an exclamation, a means of signalizing affiliation and belonging. Regardless of how different these uses appear, they're all doing the same thing: proving to their fellow men that, dude, they're chill. It's a shorthand for what Kiesling calls "homosociality," which just means platonic same-sex relationships—in other, more normal words: friends. And this space is hard for a lot of men to sustain or even to achieve. "Dude" sort of helps.

In a study Kiesling conducted in 2001 and 2002 with his graduate classes, he asked the students to record the first twenty times they heard "dude" in a period of three days. The results of this confirm what we already know to be true: By and large, men say "dude" much more than women do. However, young women are saying "dude" to one another far more than you might think—just in ways far different and more innovative than men do. Kiesling found that men generally used "dude" to greet their fellow dudes, whereas women used it in ways that were far more dexterous: to commiserate, to confront, or to tell someone what to do. It's a bid at both solidarity and distance, a paradoxical state of being that is difficult to maintain. Earnestness is, for the most part, embarrassing and not very cool at all. But "dude, I'm out" makes you feel cooler than the sum of your parts, especially because even though you're leaving the hang early to play *The Elder Scrolls IV: Oblivion* until the sun rises, you're still chill because you say "dude," like, a lot.

So much of traditional notions of masculinity seem to be

wrapped up in the idea of showmanship, peacocking, and, underneath it all, a keening desire for acceptance by men's peers. And if we think about the various cultural representations of dudes, it's sort of easy to see why that lifestyle might be appealing. In *Fast Times at Ridgemont High*, Sean Penn played Jeff Spicoli, the quintessential surfer-dude archetype who only wants to hang ten, smoke weed, and bag babes—three very important things that a teenage boy might want for himself, too. The Dude of *The Big Lebowski* has a penchant for White Russians, bowling, and bathrobes; he is perpetually unbothered and iconic enough that he inspired a religion: Dudeism, founded in 2005 by a man named Oliver Benjamin. According to an interview with CNN's Richard Ehrlich in 2013, the Church of the Latter-Day Dude is based out of Thailand and names Taoism and, yes, *The Big Lebowski* as its primary influences. And the negative traits associated with the fictional character of The Dude—the weed, the bowling, the general lack of go-get-'em—are actually not negative at all. In fact, The Dude's arc is about living life, dealing with conflict, and coexisting happily with others in a world composed mostly of crazies.

According to the religion's GeoCities-adjacent website, if you apply the "To What/From What/By What Means" method of categorizing and identifying religions, then Dudeism's similarities to Eastern philosophy emerge plainly—and naturally, if Dudeism is close enough to a preexisting, millennia-old religion, then surely, there's some credibility there. Dudeism wants to free you from the shackles of being uptight and to guide you toward a state of being described as "just taking it easy, man." The way to

**Megan C. Reynolds**

achieve Dudeism, of course, is to just be chill—"abiding" in the words of the official church. "The idea is this: Life is short and complicated, and nobody knows what to do about it," reads the website. "So don't do anything about it. Just take it easy, man." To achieve this state of being without a daily marijuana practice is extremely appealing. No wonder.

It's safe to say that "dude" is a word that only your stuffiest and most stick-up-the-ass family members or superiors would be mad about, and I will go out on a limb here and say that part of that is because its use is largely associated with men and therefore safe from much scrutiny. But even though the word is generally used by young men as a term to address their cohort, it's not gender-specific: Women use it to address one another as well as men. And while it is not yet in common circulation to address groups of people in a gender-neutral way, I have faith that in a few years, it'll get there. Much like "like," "dude" is also a discourse marker, used as a kind of shorthand for solidarity and camaraderie, and a gesture toward being down for whatever. But it's the solidarity aspect of "dude" that's by far the most interesting.

Using "like" as a discourse marker plays into women's capacity for emotional intelligence and comfort: When we hedge our speech with "like" or throw in a few definitely unnecessary "likes" to soften the blow, we are automatically doing a tiny bit of caretaking. It is an easy and nonthreatening way to make someone else feel seen and heard. I'm sure a chapter in *Men Are from Mars, Women Are from Venus* explains this much better than I will right now, but women are seen, culturally speaking, as emotional, and men are not. Women are from Venus (the planet of love, softness, and tender, goopy feelings) and men are from Mars (the manliest planet of all, the god of war, action, aggression, and no feelings at all). Not to be Susan Faludi about this, but men are perpetually in crisis. And "dude" is their small way of making a bid for connection—a teensy ask to be seen and heard by their fellow man.

The presence of "dude" builds solidarity. Imagine pulling a friend close to you at a bar and hissing sotto voce, "Dude . . ." as a mutual frenemy makes their way toward you. "Dude" is one of my favorite words to use, perhaps only second to "like" and, strangely, "verisimilitude." It's as useful as "like" and just as prevalent but receives very little of the vitriol reserved for "like"—and, by logical extension, women.

■ ■ ■

## Interlude: Girls on Film

I n the 1992 movie *My Cousin Vinny*, Joe Pesci plays a hapless personal injury attorney who just (and finally) passed the bar and somehow finds himself in the backwoods of Alabama, defending his no-good dope of a cousin in a murder trial for a crime that he and his friend clearly did not commit. Accompanying the titular cousin Vinny is Mona Lisa Vito (Marisa Tomei in an Academy Award–winning performance and arguably the style inspiration for various microtrends that the TikTok generation attributes to *The Sopranos*. Wrong! Your mob wife autumn might be inspired by Carmela, but Mona Lisa Vito was here first.). When Vinny and Lisa first show their faces in Wazoo, Alabama, it's clear in the way that movies in the nineties always were that this is a classic fish-out-of-water scenario in almost every aspect.

Vinny and Lisa are the sort of fast-talking, gum-chomping New Yorkers who I think are by now extinct in their natural habitat—the sort of people who might thud the hood of a car at a crosswalk and scream, "I'm walkin' heah!" This outer-borough charm is completely foreign to the denizens of Wazoo, and the Italian American interlopers are essentially sideshow freaks come to liven up the joint. And the party that they're starting (and eventually ending) is the murder trial, which is why Vinny and Lisa are here in the first place.

As a trial dramedy, *My Cousin Vinny* is top-notch. Vinny dresses like an out-of-work Vegas magician, a sartorial choice for which the trial judge, Chamberlain Haller, routinely finds him in contempt of court. The other issue, naturally, is that Vinny is a bit of a dummy—he's never done a trial, he barely passed the bar and, crucially, he is impersonating a lawyer named Jerry Callo, who, as we learn later, is unfortunately deceased. Over the course of the trial, Vinny is beset by various setbacks, including being fired mid-trial after declining to cross-examine any of the prosecution's witnesses during preliminary hearings. But it turns out that the brash and blunt manner that Vinny is accustomed to works well as a courtroom tactic. After discrediting two of the defense's witnesses, he's back on the case—and meets a worthy adversary in the form of FBI stuffed shirt George Wilbur, whose expert testimony about the tires of the Buick in question seems like *almost* enough to put the boys away for good.

It's pretty clear here that every person in Wazoo thinks that Vinny is not the brightest bulb due to his general incompetence, but the real linchpin upon which this case rests is sweet Mona Lisa, a woman so confident in her knowledge about car stuff and mechanics that talking about torque equals foreplay. Her attire, appearance, accent, and general countenance, which screams, "Why the fuck am I here, and if I can't leave yet, should I make the most of it?," is the very thing that sets her apart. Even though Lisa's testimony and the rest of her dialogue are strangely absent of filler words for the most part, I'd argue that "like," though ubiquitous, is West Coast–coded in a way that might be anathema to Lisa if she thought about it for a bit. It's the way she looks and how she says what she says—a Brooklyn accent that comes from the depths of Midwood, where Tomei was raised—that is the reason why everyone around her underestimates her wiles.

When Vinny finds himself in what feels and probably smells like deep shit, Lisa tries to help, offering some legal advice (she's the one who tells Vinny he can look at the prosecution's evidence), automotive expertise, and support. However, because Vinny is sleep-deprived, stressed, and a man, her attempts are rebuffed in spectacular fashion—a hissy fit of sorts that turns poisonously mean. Rightfully so, Lisa is angry, specifically because someone she cares about is going down, she can't do shit about it because Vinny won't let her, and she must defy her instincts and just sit and watch. Like another long-suffering broad and her no-good, sweet-talking fiancé, Adelaide and Nathan Detroit from *Guys and Dolls*, Lisa and Vinny are embroiled in the sort of eternal engagement endemic to fictional gangsters. (See: Christopher and Adriana's ill-fated love in *The Sopranos*.) Vinny won't marry Lisa until he wins his first case; currently, the case he is in is his first and maybe his only, and he simply refuses to take the help.

# Like

What follows is expected but still very satisfying: After some finagling, Vinny drags Lisa into the courtroom as an expert witness in automotive matters, predicated on her family's auto shop business and the fact that she's been around cars her whole life and knows a thing or two about torque, wrenches, and whatnot. The trial comes down to specifics about the tires on the Buick in question, and while the G-man's testimony is good, what's better is the evidence Lisa provides: the photos she took that Vinny carelessly dismissed as useless show some information about the tire tracks that turns out to be integral to the case. During a snippy voir dire led by the prosecution's Foghorn Leghorn–esque attorney, Lisa neatly evades any attempt to make her out to be something she's not (an idiot) by dint of her own encyclopedic knowledge of mid-century automobiles. This is only the appetizer for the delectable main course—a strangely sexually charged (is that just me?) back-and-forth on the stand with Vinny, who finally understands that the smartest thing to do here is let Lisa cook.

The monologue about Positraction, mud in the tires, and a variety of other technical car terms that mean nothing to me is iconic enough that it got Tomei an Academy Award. And while I will not assume anything about her fictional relationship with Joe Pesci in this movie, I think it's fair to say that everyone around her underestimates her just a titch, because of the way she looks, sure, but maybe because of how she sounds—and essentially who she is, too. We can look at Lisa's Positraction testimony as one of the many examples of young women using the way they speak, what they say, and how they sound to actually prove their intelligence—and to outwit the hapless men who have gravely underestimated them.

As long as the stereotypes about young women and how they speak have persisted, movies and television have tracked alongside, providing a helpful counternarrative that gives women a little more dimension and a lot more grace—essentially, the space to be real, complete people, warts and all. This is a trope that is so familiar as to be tired at this point, but let's stay here for a second. *Clueless*, perhaps the closest thing to an urtext for this kind of thing, is a classic of the genre, where Cher proves that intelligence and beauty are not mutually exclusive.

Perhaps this next admission is a bit embarrassing, but I present it in the spirit of radical transparency: There is a large gap in my cultural awareness because I was a book kid—not by choice necessarily but by circumstance, as we did not have cable growing up. This means that there are a lot of movies I have an ambient awareness of due to cultural osmosis but haven't seen, usually classics in some way or ones that everyone seems to know backward and forward and upside down. It is not surprising to me that these movies meet those criteria, but it's a nice coincidence that two films about smart women who let others think they're dumb and then use that to their advantage are in conversation with each other across time.

Perhaps experiencing them now, as I did in rapid succession, colored my takeaways a little. I worked at Jezebel, a feminist news website, for a good chunk of my career, submerging myself in the murky and tumultuous waters of online feminism and its discontents, day in and day out. The glib joke I've made in job interviews and the like is that working at Jezebel meant waking up, looking online, and seeing who or what was bad for women that day, then figuring out how to write about that in a way that felt new and refreshing. This was essentially a crash course in a brash brand of feminism where women innately understand that two things can be true at once and that, I'm sorry, the praxis is sitting in the occasional cognitive dissonance that causes. Because of this training, I can see it from both sides for the movies in question, both of which subvert the dumb-blond stereotype in their own ways. *Gentlemen Prefer Blondes* is a movie that seems anti-feminist, simply because of its time and, I guess, subject matter, but is really a cunning bit of work that demonstrates a keen understanding of the importance of securing the bag. There is nothing more feminist to me than that. And *Legally Blonde* shares a lot of its DNA; instead of a showgirl with more financial acumen than we're led to believe, we've got a sorority girl so determined to prove herself to everyone else around her that she goes to law school just to make a point. Each film gently knocks the blonds in question for how their language and appearance are "bad," but what it actually reveals is their sharp intelligence.

When *Gentlemen Prefer Blondes* premiered in 1953, Jane Russell, the film's dark-haired, husky-voiced costar, was ostensibly more well-known than Marilyn Monroe, Russell's breathy blond counterpart. Monroe had small roles in *Niagara* and *Asphalt Jungle*, but it was *Gentlemen Prefer Blondes*—in conjunction with her *Playboy* cover and her role in *How to Marry a Millionaire* in the same year—that ricocheted Monroe to the height of fame. Directed by Howard Hawks, written by Charles Lederer, and based on a stage musical and book of the same title by Anita Loos, the film received critical reception that was a bit dismissive—just a thinly veiled excuse for two attractive starlets to shimmy around in wiggle dresses and showgirl costumes for an hour and a half. In the original review in *The New York Times*, the delightfully monikered Bosley Crowther writes, "For the screenplay contrived by Mr. Lederer is less the classic saga of two smart dames, which was originally played beneath this title, than it is a silly tale of two dumb dolls."

Mr. Crowther has a point. If you look at *Gentlemen Prefer Blondes* at face value and do not engage in anything close to critical thinking, then the movie is a silly bit of fluff—a story predicated on the notion that women can only be beautiful or smart, but never both at the same time. Lorelei (Marilyn Monroe) and Dorothy (Jane Russell) are two showgirls and best friends; Lorelei is engaged to the dullard Gus Esmond, a wealthy man, and Dorothy serves as Lorelei's chaperone on a transatlantic trip to France. Unbeknownst to the two women, Esmond's father, Gus Sr., has hired Ernie Malone, a private detective, who keeps an eye on his son's floozy fiancée to potentially catch her in the act of something untoward. As a savvy woman who understands that financial independence is the key to a woman's true happiness, Lorelei quickly sets her sights on a buffoon of a man named Lord Beekman, nicknamed Piggy, who literally owns a diamond mine. (Arguably, Lorelei doesn't fall for Piggy, but rather the glittering diamond tiara brandished by his wife.)

As Lorelei busies herself with snuffling after Piggy's diamonds, Dorothy falls in quick love with Ernie Malone—only to figure out that he's spying on Lorelei because apparently she can't be trusted. Via some genuinely funny machinations, though, the women eventually get the men they want, and, because this is a movie from 1953, the natural happy ending here is marriage.

Contemporary takes on this chestnut look at Lorelei and Dorothy through a feminist lens and often find issues with it. *The Bechdel Cast*, a podcast about movies and whether they meet the Bechdel test, took on this film with their guest, author and podcaster Karina Longworth, and sniffed out the very surface-level, obvious reasons why this movie is bad for women. It promotes Western beauty standards and suggests that women are only motivated by money and will do anything to get it. While I understand and hold space for this opinion, upon watching this movie for the first time, I can't say I agree.

What stands out the most about Monroe's portrayal of Lorelei isn't just her adept physical comedy and sly timing; it's her savvy. Monroe plays Lorelei with a big, knowing wink, especially as every man in her radius is seemingly handicapped by her beauty while making incorrect assumptions about her intelligence. (I imagine that Monroe was drawing from a well of personal experience here.) Lorelei has a preternatural ability to sniff out capital and understands innately that diamonds really *are* a girl's best friend—and that their value will endure far beyond the men ensnared in her web, who are dumb enough to believe that *she's* as dumb as a box of feathers, when it's clear that she's anything but. Dorothy's attitude toward love is a little different; while Lorelei's got her eyes set on securing the bag, Dorothy prefers her men hot but poor. And there's not a whiff of competition between the two as they embark on their slapstick overseas voyage—both women are set on different men and are willing to help each other out, knowing full well that if they play the game right, these hapless idiots—and what they each truly desire—will fall right into their laps.

Throughout the entire movie, it's clear to the audience that the women are the smart ones in this equation but parlay the assumption that they're not into situations that benefit them. Dorothy, who I think as a "feminist" I am supposed to identify with, has something akin to a moral compass and a sick dedication to the idea of love for love's sake—compatibility trumping money every time. (It's important to note here that Dorothy is horny, enough so to sing "Ain't There Anyone Here for Love" while strolling through a gymnasium full of men in nude boy shorts, and crucially Lorelei is not.) Lorelei understands that there's a version of happiness (and freedom) in financial security, and if playing dumb with a hint of earnestness means marrying some old man who's just happy to be there, then why not? Doesn't everyone deserve happiness? Why should we be worried about how they get there?

If the film's self-awareness doesn't feel clear, consider Lorelei's thesis statement, "Diamonds Are a Girl's Best Friend," which is by far one of the most insane and spectacular displays I have seen in a long time—melodramatic and weirdly kinky in a way that feels maybe subversive for its time. The light fixtures, a chandelier and candelabra, are literally made of women dressed in black latex swimsuits and matching caps holding torches aloft. A sea of chorus boys, rejected by Lorelei at the top of the number, pretends to shoot themselves en masse and then rises—zombies brought back to life via song and Monroe's animal magnetism in the iconic pink dress we are all by now familiar with. And in the song, Lorelei's fiancé, Mr. Esmond, who's watching this number from the audience, is thoroughly roasted, dragged, tarred, and feathered. How did he get there, you ask, and why? Pointless questions! It's useless to look for much logic in the plot of any movie musical. Pretend that it makes sense that Lorelei's fiancé, accompanied by his father, somehow hustled their way to France for this confrontation at the end, where Lorelei delivers her climactic monologue to Gus Sr., who thinks he has her number. Of course she doesn't want to marry Gus for his money, but for the money he's going to get when Gus Sr. dies. "I want to marry him for *your* money!" Lorelei says—a statement that finally gets through. "They told me you were stupid," he says. "You don't sound so stupid to me."

Monroe's retort is sharp and to the point. "I can be smart when it's important, but most men don't like it," she says—a truth that feels almost universal, and a theme that's explored with verve some fifty years later. *Legally Blonde*, a 2001 film that is now a feminist classic, takes a lot of lessons from its spiritual predecessor, and the results are, sorry to say, iconic.

Reese Witherspoon is Elle Woods, a seemingly vapid sorority girl with a penchant for pink who, at the movie's start, thinks she is on the precipice of an engagement with Warner (Matthew Davis), her drip of a boyfriend. Though it is obvious, what transpires at the supposed engagement dinner is the opposite: Elle's heel turn comes when her slimy boyfriend dumps her at the fancy restaurant because, as he says, "I need a Jackie, not a Marilyn." In short, Elle's the kind of girl who's here for a good time, not a long time, and certainly not marriage material for anyone on the Senate track, as this man seems to be. Warner's first stop before the Senate is Harvard Law. Even though Elle says, with some accuracy, "Law school is for people who are boring and ugly and serious," and she is none of those things at all, she sets her sights on getting into Harvard Law, too, to prove to Warner first, then ultimately herself, that she can. And after scoring a 179 on her LSAT and submitting a sizzle reel instead of an application essay that ends with her emerging from a pool in a bikini, the admissions board of Harvard Law—a group of white men dazzled by both her appearance and her audacity—let her in.

What's a little galling is how dated this movie feels, some twenty years after the fact. I understand that the reaction to Elle's presentation, in all its hyperfeminine, bimbo glory, is hammed up to highlight the fish-out-of-water situation, but it is as if these people have never encountered a blond woman with a strong personal aesthetic who happens to be smart. But the way Elle looks and, on some level, acts is reason for almost everyone she runs into to underestimate her. Even the tiniest of setbacks stokes the fire under Elle Woods's ass. She is not afraid of a challenge.

The challenge for Elle throughout the entire movie seems to be just existing; everyone is breathtakingly rude to Elle, right to her face. "Hey, maybe there's, like, a sorority you could join instead, like" is how one law student chooses to make fun of Elle after she asks to join their study group—nice try at an insult, but, also, just rude? Another scene finds Elle dressed like a Playboy Bunny at a party when everyone else is in their civvies—a popular trope in movies at the turn of this century. Elle's bunny costume moment mimics Bridget Jones showing up to a tarts and vicars party in full skank, having missed the memo that the tarts and vicars part was canceled. Warner, the good-for-nothing boyfriend now engaged to Vivian (Selma Blair), physically and aesthetically Elle's opposite, tells Elle multiple times that she's not smart enough for law school and that she needs to do "something more valuable with her time," but never actually says what. In fact, the only person who doesn't treat her like an idiot is Emmett (Luke Wilson), a TA to the mean and stern Professor Callahan (an appropriately dour Victor Garber), who spends most of the movie underestimating Elle's intelligence, then attempting to coerce her into a sexual encounter in exchange for power. It's as if every single person in Elle's trajectory thinks she's dumb as rocks—and she lets them think that, until the time is right to reveal her intelligence. Elle is not stupid; she has a sharp tongue, a quick wit, and the kind of brain that really absorbs information, whether it's about fabric or evidentiary support. Every teacher looks surprised when they discover that she can retain information, and even though her delivery is her own—a little ditzy, very bubbly—her answers are right.

It is not unreasonable to think that a woman could dress like a Barbie doll but have the brains of a hard-boiled criminal attorney—but what Elle has that some of the other characters in this movie don't is *emotional* intelligence. When speaking to Brooke (Ali Larter), a fitness influencer and sorority sister on trial for the murder of her rich (and much older) husband, Elle's strategy is to lean into her soft skills first—to get on Brooke's level, she arrives at the prison with a care basket stocked with, among other things, issues of "the Bible," *Cosmopolitan* magazine. Elle's ability to earn Brooke's trust gets her the one thing all the supposedly smart men surrounding her could not—Brooke's alibi, which turns out to be unnecessary. Elle's in-depth knowledge of proper perm aftercare is enough to win the case, setting Brooke free. (The alibi, if you must know, is that she was getting lipo at the time of the murder, and that is an embarrassing admission for a fitness influencer.)

*Legally Blonde* lets Reese Witherspoon do some of her best acting work, second only to the 2013 video where she tipsily yells, "Do you know who I am?" at an Atlanta cop who clearly doesn't when she and her then-husband Jim Toth are pulled over for a traffic stop; Witherspoon was eventually arrested for disorderly conduct after getting out of the car not once but twice, in defiance of the police officer's orders. (Please find this video if you can. Listening to Reese Witherspoon go full Karen, screaming, "You're about to find out who I am!" is satisfying in a way that I can't quite explain. It's certainly not her finest moment, but for me, it is.) In her hands, Elle Woods is smarter than the average bear but doesn't let anyone else in on the joke until she's good and ready. "A blond is powerful. You hold more cards than you think you do," Emmett tells her—he's the only man who takes her seriously, just as she is. Please remember that the entire point of Elle's law school journey was to prove to a man that she could do it so that he would love her more—not the best reason but not the worst, for people have done far stupider things for love. But when Warner, ever the opportunist, comes sniffing back around in light of Elle's courtroom success, he is soundly rejected, as unlucky in life as he is in love. That's what you get for judging a book by its cover.

Of course women can be both beautiful and intelligent, and we have learned by now (for the most part) that people are more than the sum of their physical presentation—the clothes they wear and the way they speak. This trope will prevail in the culture in one form or another because watching it be invalidated is so satisfying—and it will perpetuate because, like all stereotypes, there's a tiny kernel of truth at its heart. Just because we understand both intellectually and practically that the way a woman speaks has anything to do with her intelligence doesn't mean that we always put that understanding into practice. Half the work of proper communication is really listening to what the other person is saying and divorcing how they're saying it from the actual meaning or intent. This is sad but also a little true: People really do think that women speak the way that they do because they're stupid, and sadly, for all those who operate under that misconception, they're proven wrong almost every time.

## Interlude: How Do People Learn English?

It's no mistake that the bulk of this book is largely concerned with American English and how it evolves and changes over time, and that's due to one very simple fact: Context matters. I was born in the United States and therefore speak American English, because, aside from a brief few years in my childhood when my father assured me that my first language was Mandarin Chinese (my mother's native tongue), I was raised in an English-speaking household.

Despite the fact that my sister Jenny and I heard English for most of the year, when we lived with my father, summers spent with my mother in California weren't multilingual. My mother spoke Chinese as often as she needed to, and in the Bay Area in the mid-nineties, there were plenty of opportunities. She "charmed" the hostesses at various restaurants and used her outside voice on the phone to her family in Taipei. My two younger sisters, Tessa and Shaina (half sisters, if we're being technical, but I am not) went to Chinese school on the week-ends and, at various points in their lives, were sent to live in Taipei with my mother's family—an ersatz language immersion program, if only because everyone around them spoke Mandarin, so they had to keep up. My sister Jenny and I don't know enough Mandarin to do anything useful, but I like to tell myself and anyone who is listening that I can sort of understand it.

To be clear—any actual facility I have with Mandarin is due to context. I can tell when my mother is talking about her children, but usually, she's gesticulating in our general direction. Despite my actual inability to, say, ask where the bathroom is in Mandarin, spending time around a native speaker occasionally influences the way I talk. If I'm with my mother and am not particularly annoyed at her at that moment and she's holding something that I might want to eat, I will say, "Let me see see that scone." This isn't because I'm a child, but because "Ràng wǒ kàn kàn," which is the same sentence in Mandarin, repeats the verb "kàn," "to see," and in my brain, that's nice. (The reason why is simple—repeating a verb in Mandarin indicates that you want to try to do something and suggests effort.) My sisters and I will say this to one another in our group chat or in person, too. This manner of speaking is definitely English but informed by our personal context—in this case, our mother, who will also ask to see see something because, I guess, that turn of phrase is endemic to the women in my immediate family. But if I were to ask a friend to let me see see the $756 dress she doesn't think she should buy but ultimately will, I imagine that on some level, she'd wonder if I have incurred brain damage and what, if anything, she can do to help.

This is technically and actually a nonstandard use of English, and one that I hardly imagine will take off—but it is unique to me, my family, and my identity, just like my use of "like" and other filler words are. And if I've done anything close to a good job so far, it's clear that using "like" in the way that this book covers is a uniquely American tic. "I wonder if they teach this in ESL classes," a man I found in the dregs of a dating app once typed to me when I mentioned that I was writing a book about this very subject. (I didn't deign to meet this person, who shared with me that he was about to watch a collection of experimental documentary shorts from the 1960s, mostly because there's nothing I'd rather do less than that. However, I thank him for bringing up this pertinent point , which is worthy of attention, and hope that he's found whatever he was looking for. It certainly wasn't me.)

Consulting a few resources aimed at teaching non-native speakers how to speak English proves that the experimental film aficionado had a point—ESL classes are geared toward teaching people how to speak English in a professional capacity and not like a native speaker who knows the secret language of filler words and interjections and how to use them properly. Thankfully, I have two primary sources in my own life who were able to provide a little more context.

My mother moved to the United States in 1981 and has lived here ever since, bouncing around from the Bay Area to the Pacific Northwest, stopping briefly in Albuquerque and then, for reasons my sisters and I will never quite understand, leaving the desert behind for the rolling countryside of North Carolina, some forty minutes outside of Raleigh. Even though she's lived in this country for over forty years, she hasn't lost her accent, and she speaks English not quite like a native speaker but well enough to my ear that I hardly register her accent or syntax as foreign.

She learned English the way many immigrants do—first, formally, in school, and then practically, by surrounding herself with native speakers. Some of the aforementioned native speakers included the casts of both *Happy Days* and *Leave It to Beaver*, two shows that she watched growing up in Taipei. "TV is more entertaining," she said. "What we learned at school could be dead boring." That foundation, combined with time spent in various pockets of this country, means that she still speaks with the formality that so many ESL speakers do—not because she's a particularly formal person (not by a long shot), but because this is how she learned and, as my sisters and I figured out a while ago, you really can't teach an old dog new tricks.

My cousin Winnie, born and raised between Taipei and Canada, is a different story. When my family and I went to Taiwan in 2019 for the first time in almost twenty years, Winnie dutifully led her big American cousins around, switching seamlessly from Mandarin to American-accented English that is probably better than mine. "I learned English naturally by being immersed in an English-speaking environment," she says. "It started with my mom playing Disney English every day for me starting at three, and growing up watching Disney Channel shows in English. Then at seven, moving to Canada and attending school in an all-Canadian environment. The biggest help with being able to speak English fluently is consistent usage, whether being in Taiwan or abroad."

Winnie also picked up English by watching a lot of YouTube—vlogs, mostly—as a natural complement to the English she was learning in school. "That experience is way different than learning English in school, because I watched a lot of vlogs," she says. "Hosts speak naturally, and there's a lot of improv. In school, it's goal-oriented: getting directions, for business, and for formal usage. Even in conversation classes, foreign teachers are not encouraged to focus on filler words or slang."

It's not quite a surprise that ESL classes are geared toward goals and action—English is the language of international commerce, after all—but it is a bit of a disappointment. And a lot of the world tries to mimic American speech, thanks to the proliferation of our media; if my mother and my cousin were both watching American sitcoms and the like during their respective childhoods, then I'd bet a dollar and a doughnut that they are not alone. And, happily, my hunch is correct. According to a 2021 article in *The New York Times*, the pals who hung out at Central Perk for ten seasons of television have served as de facto English tutors to people around the world. *Friends*, that innocuous, imminently watchable cultural touchstone is "a near perfect-amalgam of easy-to-understand English and real-life scenarios that feel familiar even to people who live worlds away from Manhattan's West Village," Mike Ives writes. Assimilation isn't the desired outcome—but people are watching *Friends* around the world, as the show is and will be in syndication until the end of the world, and are therefore absorbing American mannerisms, idioms, and expressions.

■ ■ ■

## Interlude: Nǐ Shuō Shénme?!

To keep it 100, if you ask me if I speak Chinese, the answer is generally "not really," despite a solid few months with HelloChinese, an app on my phone that I downloaded before a trip to Taiwan in 2019 and haven't really used since. My Mandarin is essentially nonexistent, but I've spent enough time around the language that to be in the presence of native speakers is soothing, even though an enthusiastic conversation in Mandarin can sound like a heated argument. Again, I am not saying in writing or otherwise that I can reasonably speak or understand the language, but its cadences are familiar to me and create otherwise pleasant background noise in places like the nail salon, where Sofi, the owner, and her sister talk among themselves and their cohort. There are some words and phrases I do understand, usually concerning money or food. And a word that I hear frequently enough in these conversations is a filler word that's so commonly used that it doesn't even register— "nèi ge." It's a useful phrase, and the context where I hear the word is usually crammed in the middle of a rapid-fire sentence my mother's whisper-screaming at one of her sisters on the phone.

"Nèi ge" roughly translates to "that" in English, but in spoken Mandarin, it slots into a conversation or sentence in the same way "like" can. A paper written by Aiqing Wang, professor of linguistics at the University of Liverpool, delves into the backstory of "nèi ge" and its use as a discourse marker. Wang also touches on "zhe ge," which is closely linked to "nèi ge" and functions very similarly but is also used as a means of emphasis. ("Zhe gi she wo de," which means roughly "*This* one is mine," a phrase I can hear my mother saying so clearly in my head, carries a little more impact now.)

"Nèi ge" is a demonstrative pronoun that endured the process of grammaticalization, just like "like," and is now a discourse marker that is as versatile, if not more so, than its English counterpart. "Nèi ge" and its more formal iteration, "na ge," are useful tools to "introduce topics, change subjects, and preserve face," Wang writes. Which version of the word you choose to say is also a means of signifying positions of power: "'Na ge' is deployed to mark discourses taking place between interlocutors of an equal status or those addressing listeners in a superior position." This consideration for status, along with the idea that a filler word can help you save face, demonstrates just how vital these words are to communication. If you start to pay attention when people are speaking Mandarin around you, you will hear this word time and time again. It has also not escaped my attention that to American ears the word itself sounds a lot like the N-word in a way that could set off alarm bells in polite company.

In August 2020, Professor Gregory Patton said a word on a Zoom call that nearly cost him his career. Patton is a professor at the University of Southern California's Marshall School of Business—one of the top twenty business schools according to the gold standards for such things, the *U.S. News* rankings of the best grad schools in the country. (Perhaps you remember this list from senior year of high school, if you were the kind of student concerned with where your college ranked and what effect that would have on your education and therefore the rest of your life.) During this presentation, which was for a communications class, Patton was discussing the use of filler words and how utterances like "um" and "er" should be avoided in business communications. Patton thoughtfully started mentioning words in other languages so as to be more inclusive of his international students. "In China, the common word is 'that'—that, that, that, that," he said in Mandarin. Unfortunately for Patton, who repeated the word multiple times in rapid succession as a means of demonstrating the word's versatility and intended use, if you say "nèi ge" and your accent isn't that great, the word sounds a little bit like another word that is definitely not acceptable in polite society or otherwise.

Patton's use of "nèi ge"—again, a filler word that is ubiquitous in Chinese and roughly one hundred miles removed from the word it sort of sounds like—caused ire among some of his students and prompted a complaint filed to the school's administration about the incident in question, sparking a brief but hot conflagration that feels like just another example of current college campus PC culture gone just a teensy bit haywire. In the letter, where Patton was accused of negligence, a collective of students wrote, "This phrase, clearly and precisely before instruction, is always identified as a phonetic homonym and a racial derogatory term, and should be carefully used, especially in the context of speaking Chinese within the social context of the United States. The way we heard it in class was indicative of a much more hurtful word with tremendous implications for the Black community."

The university administration's response to this, from Marshall School Dean Geoffrey Garrett in an email shared with CNN, is the sort of head-scratcher that leaves me wondering if the kids—or the campus administrators terrified of the specter of campus cancel culture—actually *are* all right.

"Professor Greg Patton repeated several times a Chinese word that sounds very similar to a vile racial slur in English," Garrett's missive read. "Understandably, this caused great pain and upset among students, and for that I am deeply sorry. It is simply unacceptable for faculty to use words in class that can marginalize, hurt and harm the psychological safety of our students. We must and we will do better."

Patton was replaced by a different instructor for the class for the duration of the semester and issued his own apology sometime after the incident, saying he was sorry for causing anyone "discomfort and pain" during his lesson. According to Patton, he used "nèi ge" as an example in response to some of his international students' suggestions to highlight words in other languages and to essentially be *more* inclusive of his students' various backgrounds. "I had not realized this negativity previously or I would have replaced the example as we now have," Patton wrote—the rare public apology that wasn't actually warranted. Or was it?

At *The Atlantic*, Conor Friedersdorf's investigation into this incident produced a letter from an anonymous student that provided some insight into the way the new generation thinks. "Can you expect a student to focus or feel safe after hearing a word that sounds like a racial slur? To tell my Black classmates that they shouldn't be offended by something is objectively wrong. . . . My place is to support them," the student wrote. "We don't say a certain onomatopoeia around Asian people because one word is also a racial slur. Just don't say words that sound like racial slurs—it isn't that complicated." (The word in question here is "chink," as in a "chink in your armor." In 2012 ESPN.com published an article about Taiwanese basketball player Jeremy Lin, who was playing for the Knicks at the time. The entirety of New York City basketball fans was gripped in Linsanity; after the Knicks lost against the New Orleans Hornets early in the season after a winning streak, the article about the game was headlined "Chink in the Armor," next to a photo of Lin. Bad move! People don't say it that often anymore, but also it is not a word or turn of phrase that is essential to everyday speech, so if I must, it's apples and oranges here.)

On the opposite end of this spectrum, CC Chen, a student at USC, started a Change.org petition to reinstate Patton, writing that for Patton "to be censored simply because a Chinese word sounds like an English pejorative term is a mistake and is not appropriate, especially given the educational setting. It also dismisses the fact that Chinese is a real language and has its own pronunciations that have no relation to English."

Once the incident made its way through the cycle of public litigation via think pieces, many tweets, and a segment on *The Daily Show*, the general consensus was that this incident is yet another example of how difficult it is to both be a student and also a teacher on a college campus in the 2020s, as college administrations around the country try to adjust to changing social mores around what is politically correct.

I won't be the one to tell you how to feel about this issue, though I hope my stance is clear: The brouhaha surrounding Patton is ridiculous, though, as a Libra, I suppose I can see a little bit of the other side, having once found myself in a situation spiritually similar to what Patton endured. One of my sister's friends, a Black woman who has known my family (including my mother) since childhood, saw a video of my mother making dumplings in my kitchen. The details are lost to the sands of time, but when my mother said "nèi ge" a few times in the middle of her narration, we clarified quickly that the word she was saying was not what it sounded like. The friend understood, my mother kept talking, and, if I remember right, my sisters and I ate the dumplings in relative peace.

For students learning English, filler words are generally not part of the curriculum, except as examples of what not to do in speech. But when learning Mandarin in the very same way— from a course structured to teach how to speak the language like a native—filler words like "nèi ge" are taught, because without them, you will inevitably sound like an overly formal robot. The function of filler words across languages is the same—just like an "um" or a "like" buys you time or gives you a minute to think while you're in the middle of a conversation, "nèi ge" does the same thing. It fills the pauses between disparate thoughts in a sentence and signposts that the information that follows is difficult to say and important. And it is because of the way fillers allow for a little grace that they are taught to non-native speakers as a small kindness—a gift that aids clarity and communication.

"Filler words are definitely worth learning for several reasons. The first reason is because, well, you need them," reads a blog post on the website for Yoyo Chinese, a reputable online language program that promises to teach you conversational Chinese in six months or less. "You need them even more in Chinese than you do in your native language, because you need extra time to think before you speak." There are seemingly as many primers for how to properly use filler words in Mandarin as there are for how *not* to use filler words in English. And across these various resources, "nèi ge" shows up as the most important filler word for non-native speakers looking to sound authentic, because almost everyone uses it all the time.

It never occurred to me that these phrases were grammatically optional, like filler words are, because any understanding I have at all about how to speak Mandarin came not from a textbook but from a native speaker—my mother, hello, Mom, once more. I've heard "nèi ge" more times than I can count, glossing over it as I listen to an illegible conversation, assuming (correctly) that it is an essential part of speech due to frequency of use and repetition. It's this filler word that is the closest analogue to "like," fitting into sentences where you'd otherwise let dead air fill the space between thoughts—and especially when what you're about to say is difficult, delicate, or possibly hurtful (unintentionally, but still).

A YouTube lesson about the proper usage of filler words in conversational Chinese offers some clarity. In the video, the instructor, Angel, playing two speakers, engages in a series of alarming personal conversations to demonstrate how to use a filler word, but, most importantly, why. It turns out that, just like in English, filler words do a lot of work to soften or temper the impact of a sentence on its unsuspecting target. The scenarios are uncomfortable, but I'd argue one is more so than the other. In both conversations, Angel 1 brings up two sensitive subjects—first, to ask for money that she's owed and, second, arguably worse, to tell the other person (Angel 1 as Angel 2, playing both roles with verve) that she's gained weight. Each example conversation starts with a stutter; as the person asking the question, Angel 1 hedges, hems, and haws, uttering almost every filler word she can before Angel 2 asks her(self) to simply get to the point and spit it out.

Reading through the list of examples provided by each website I found was far more useful for me to figure out how these words were used. As I whispered the example sentences out loud, my accent basically nonexistent, I realized that my Mandarin is horrible, and at times I found myself too embarrassed to continue with the sentence, even though the only person paying attention was the cat. It is generous to say that any of these phrases sounded correct tonally or otherwise—I assure you, they did not. What I did notice, though, is that the filler words were inserted where they felt natural, because that's the Mandarin I'm used to hearing—my mother patiently telling a teenager at the boba shop in Taipei about her four daughters, visiting from America, and how they'd like their tea. You can't pay me any amount of money to accurately translate what my mother says in these interactions—that's not the point. It's the way the language sounds—without filler words, the familiar turns foreign.

## Chapter 6

# That's, Like, Not Very Professional

George Cukor's beautiful, three-hour-long musical *My Fair Lady* is beloved as a classic of the genre by many, though upon my first couple viewings of the film, I found myself wondering why. Based on the 1913 play *Pygmalion* by George Bernard Shaw, *My Fair Lady* at its heart is a tale as old as time: A man who thinks he knows a woman better than she knows herself turns out to be wrong. Personally, not even Cecil Beaton's luscious sets and costumes could make this film palatable enough for me to watch all the way through—blame my attention span, which is due home from war any day now, and also my tolerance for the story itself (vaguely sexist, romantic-ish, largely pedantic?). Truthfully, I sat down to watch *My Fair Lady* on a hazy Saturday evening, looking for something long and involved and ideally somewhat soothing, and instead of relaxing, I discovered that Eliza Doolittle's triumphant tale contained some lessons that could be useful for this book. But also, generally, for life.

Henry Higgins (Rex Harrison) first encounters Eliza Doolittle (Audrey Hepburn) selling flowers out of a basket in the sopping rain. Theatergoers in fancy dress walk around her like she's an obstacle to be avoided—and while I do think this is rude, I sort of understand why. Eliza Doolittle is of the streets, and so the accent, volume, and tone of her voice, meant to be Cockney, is extraordinarily insane, like a caricature of a Dickensian orphan or a particularly enthusiastic cast member of *Oliver!*. She shrieks, caterwauls, and is relatively incomprehensible, but regardless of how unrefined this might sound, one has to salute her for being truly, completely herself. (This analysis of Eliza may seem unnecessarily rude to Hepburn, but I assure you that it is necessary to really, fully understand what we are working with here.)

Now for the story: Higgins, a professor of phonetics, is lurking about the theater, too, using his one party trick to wow the crowd first before pecking his way toward Eliza, which is that he can tell where someone is from, down to the village, just from the way they speak. This trick delights Colonel Pickering (Wilfrid Hyde-White), one of the aforementioned theater attendees just trying to get home. Pickering is a retired naval officer, an author of a book about Sanskrit, and, also, a linguist—quite the dilettante. These men bond over a shared love of "proper" English, of the sort spoken by people who look and sound like them, and then turn their attention to an interesting project: to see if they can transform Eliza Doolittle from a ruddy-cheeked street urchin who drops her *h*'s to a lady of society, *just* to see if it can be done.

A note: This plan isn't necessarily communicated to Eliza. Instead, Higgins dangles a carrot via a rude suggestion that's also probably true: If she sounds less like a Dickensian orphan and more like a marchioness, she can advance her career by moving from selling flowers on the street to selling them in a shop. Beyond that, the world is her oyster. God forbid Eliza actually be good at selling flowers simply how she is (though there is no evidence that supports this), because she will surely be much better if her speech and communication sound less like herself and more like whatever the gatekeepers of Edwardian London think is right.

Lured by the prospect of climbing this corporate ladder, Eliza winds up at Higgins's doorstep, in search of help. And what transpires afterward is predictable enough. After a fair amount of histrionics and shrieking resistance, Eliza succumbs to Higgins's teachings, breaking free from the patterns of speech and behavior that were holding her back and, in what we are supposed to view as a moment of triumph, fooling polite society into thinking that she is one of them.

Since Higgins is a professor of phonetics, his main issue with Eliza's general comportment is not the way she dresses or the fact that she could use a hot bath—two issues that are quickly remedied by the no-nonsense household staff. He's very concerned with the ungodly, inhuman, and altogether incorrect way she speaks. Eliza's speech is peppered with slang, grammatically incorrect, and, in Hepburn's interpretation, very shrill and full of dramatics for *absolutely no reason.*

"It's 'ow' and 'garn' that keep her in her place!" Higgins says, suggesting that if she does not succumb to his plan, she'll be condemned to a life lived on the fringes of proper and acceptable society—all that potential, doomed to wither in obscurity. The implication, of course, is that this one thing is holding her back, and no one will take her seriously as a professional floral vendor and possible future florist if she sounds like who she really is.

Though I find almost everything about Henry Higgins's entire deal to be annoying and not very kind, I do see some of his point, as much as it kills me to say it. You'd be hard-pressed to find much criticism of Audrey Hepburn's body of work, but I don't think it's controversial to say that she's not a comedic genius. This is evident in her portrayal of Eliza Doolittle—but even though her affect is grating and also confounding, Hepburn's Eliza has a zany streak and a real, uninhibited lust for life. Prior to her behavioral and linguistic glow-up, Eliza scrabbles around Higgins's beautifully appointed home like Gollum in a petticoat, shrieking and howling for little legitimate reason—a walking id, like when Bella in Yorgos Lanthimos's *Poor Things* discovers masturbation and simply cannot stop fucking herself with whatever phallic-shaped object she finds. There's an enviable sort of freedom in both women that's vaguely appealing—though, again, I don't understand why Hepburn screams so much as Eliza. The *only* reason must be because Hepburn wanted to really drive home that Eliza Doolittle is truly, really, desperately in need of help.

When I watched this movie not once but twice, as I did first for leisure and then, begrudgingly, for this book you hold in your hands, what stood out the most was just how much of an asshole Henry Higgins is—terrifically sexist, boorish, but occasionally charming. On its face, the *Pygmalion* plot is an archetype of a particular kind of romantic comedy, as seen in movies like *She's All That* and, more earnestly, the third season of Netflix's *Bridgerton*, when Colin Bridgerton falls in love with Penelope Featherington as he grooms her to become a viable prospect on the marriage market. But if you peek under the hood here, something else becomes clear. *My Fair Lady* is a story about an abstract and changing notion that influences everything we do in our careers: that of professionalism, and whether or not it matters at all.

Prior to the pandemic, the idea of being professional was heavily predicated on interpersonal, face-to-face interactions, as well as verbal and written communication. Being a professional in the workplace is a skill that doesn't come naturally. According to a pamphlet aimed at teenagers and created by the United States Department of Labor, professionalism is a soft skill: "Professionalism does not mean wearing a suit or carrying a briefcase; rather, it means conducting oneself with responsibility, integrity, accountability, and excellence," it reads. "It means communicating effectively and appropriately and always finding a way to be productive."

In the years before the pandemic, there was a baseline expectation of professionalism in the workplace, but the contours of this varied by environment. A general manager of a coffee shop who acts like the titular character in *The Boss Baby* is merely performing professionalism that isn't quite right for that specific environment. But if we are to look at the US Department of Labor's definition—which is ostensibly fed to the next generation so that they might feel comfortable and competent enough to lay us all off—then things get trickier. This is in part because the characteristics of professionalism can be subjective. My idea of what "integrity" means might differ from yours, and that, my pals, is the problem with this entire enterprise. Like Emily Post acolytes who are sticklers for "etiquette"—public-facing behavior that is the social equivalent of professionalism—I believe being professional actually means just doing well at your job and leaving work where it belongs, which is at the office and, if you can help it, nowhere near your home.

But the physical boundary that separated work from home eroded when the pandemic forced a large part of the global workforce to become indoor cats for a little while, kick-starting several strange and uncertain months when people Cloroxed their groceries and their entire lives were confined to where they lived and with whom. The pandemic's sudden onset and the general miasma of anxiety and virus added a tremendous amount of stress to some of the most stressful and important jobs—those of essential workers, whose work was indeed so essential that they had to do it outside of the home. For the rest of us assholes with Slack jobs—"bullshit jobs" as David Graeber calls them—we dutifully banged our pots and pans at night and figured out that a lot of what we were doing at work was a tremendous waste of time.

Office jobs are annoying for a very few dumb little reasons, but none as infuriating as the expectation that when you're on the company clock, you're working and your time is not yours. Scrolling endless pages of the internet looking for shoes,

**Megan C. Reynolds**

googling "best plunger broken toilet," or moderating a subreddit about guinea pigs are all acceptable uses of time on the company clock, especially if you've figured out that your time is *always yours*, even when it sometimes, temporarily belongs to someone else. Were I ever to find myself in a managerial role, I would make it known that I truly don't care how the day is spent—everyone is an adult and therefore can be trusted to be responsible for their own time.

But being in a physical space with other people, in a row of cubicles under flickering fluorescents or elbow-to-elbow in a god-awful open office, exerts a little pressure to at least try to look productive when someone walks by.

If I take a very serious look at my career, I'd say that I'm professional when it counts and a regular person in all the other instances when it really doesn't. Over email I am a chipper ray of sunshine, thanks to my embarrassing millennial overuse of exclamation points as a means of signaling how nice, friendly, and enthusiastic I'd like to be seen. In front of a group, presenting one to three slides from a PowerPoint, I am (hopefully) more adroit in my speech and am able to convey competence and intelligence with not just what I'm saying but how. This approach has not yet failed me. But perhaps my habit of saying "fuck" a lot on Slack when talking to my coworkers is the thing that's holding me back from someday being the CEO of something. Maybe there's some value in being "professional"; maybe my career would have gone in an entirely different direction.

Even though I find nothing wrong with the way I act in the workplace and have yet to be spoken to about it by any superiors, I can still recognize that it probably doesn't gel with a layperson's understanding of "professionalism." And "postpandemic," I realized that I'd spent a majority of my career insistently acting as if professionalism didn't matter. I needed some help understanding what it even meant in the first place.

Samara Bay, author of *Permission to Speak: How to Change What Power Sounds Like, Starting with You*, is a dialect and accent coach and public speaking advisor. When I turned to her for guidance, she immediately understood my poorly stated question about professionalism and its discontents. It turns out that the reason why I've carried a teensy complex about my personal notions of professionalism and how they do or do not square with what is expected is another issue brought about by men.

"I love professionalism to actually mean that you're a professional," she said. "I think in interpersonal, low-stakes conversations, if we're judging people's voices based on how much they sound like rich white men have historically sounded, we are quite frankly fucking ourselves for the type of work environment we want to have in the future."

There are actually two different types of professionalism, Bay told me, validating what I have always thought to be true. There's the professionalism of the low-stakes and quotidian face-to-face situations, where we figure out how to coexist in the same space and to speak a language that is familiar and specific to the environment. In short, all this is, is being a decent person, treating others how you'd like to be treated, and, above all, operating with the tacit understanding that a job is just a job and not your entire personality. And then there's the "professionalism" one might summon for important events, like board meetings, shareholder presentations, and anything involving a lectern. Understanding the differences between the two iterations is crucial. I have a pretty good grasp on both, but a quick scan through my emails over the course of any week reveals an insane truth: I use "like" over *email*, at work, in precisely the way I'd say it out loud, and it's clear to me that I'm doing it to communicate that I am professional but still, somehow, cool and normal. Is *this* professional, or is this just a weird attempt by a middle-aged woman to seem like she's mature when it counts and slightly immature when it doesn't?

As Bay and I talked, it became clearer to me that my questions about filler words, professionalism, and sounding like—I'm so sorry—a boss were actually about confidence, self-assuredness, and authenticity.

"If we have done the work to believe that what we're talking about matters and that we deserve to be here, we will actually use fewer filler words," Bay said. "So they're less good or bad and more an indication of whether or not you believe you have the authority to be there. And that's why fillers mess with us. But if we do the inner work to be like, 'Damn, thank god for them that I'm here with my point of view and my experience,' we will inevitably say 'like' less, and the filler words that are there are there because they help."

Bay's book puts into words a feeling I've always known to be true for myself but have never been able to articulate: The idea that our speech has to convey the formality associated with work—whether it be walking to the kitchen to get some coffee or presenting the aforementioned deck to the CEO, CMO, and COO (for good measure)—is a myth. "This myth may be stopping you from giving yourself permission to show up authentically in work contexts where it's authenticity, actually, that would seal the deal," she writes. In short, if you are as close to yourself as possible as is appropriate or comfortable for public spaces and mixed company, the confidence that comes from feeling like who you are is good enough will come through, no matter what you're saying or how—filler words and all.

One area of professional speech that I assumed Bay would have issue with when we spoke is that of corporate jargon, a dense language all its own that is, by and large, endemic to the modern office and (thankfully) nowhere else. Jargon, Bay told me, is useful because it's one specific and universal language for that environment. Logically, this makes sense, but practically, corporate robospeak is extremely idiomatic and creates a sense of distance from the subject at hand. Telling Marjorie you'll circle back but you might not have the bandwidth is a tidy shorthand for saying that you don't have the time or desire to deal with that thing right now but will do it later, you swear. Marjorie knows what I mean, *I* said what I said, and, most importantly, a complex meaning was conveyed with very little—and I didn't even have to use a filler word or three to get my point across. Marjorie understands that when I say I will circle back, I'm setting a boundary as well as an expectation of when she can expect some of my time. In other environments, this sort of care in communication is better known as being considerate or just not being an asshole. I suppose we are blessed to have an entire dictionary of words that, once learned, will allow you to be kind in the workplace in a way that everyone else expects and understands.

Blessedly, the majority of office work now, after the pandemic debunked the fiction that being physically in the same space as your coworkers is somehow better for productivity, takes place in written communication, from emails to Slacks to text messages during the day when you need to talk shit about something annoying and don't want Big Brother to read it. Working from home erases the need to speak out loud during the day, which is a blessing. Following Bay's logic that if you are confident in what you're saying as you're saying it and therefore filler words will be naturally absent from your speech, one assumes that anytime you *do* have to talk out loud, you've had some time to prepare. But generally, we don't have to talk out loud to anyone if we don't want to, so the risk of sounding like, I don't know, a, like, functionally incompetent dummy is low. But other jobs are more customer-facing; medical professionals, lawyers, law enforcement, and the like all take oaths that they should uphold. The professionalism that's appropriate for their jobs is baked into the contracts, and as these jobs require talking to lots of people in situations that are often uncomfortable, decent bedside manners go a long way.

If you'll join me on this stretch of the imagination, though, doctors, dentists, police officers, and your cousin Mark, the personal injury attorney, aren't the only professionals with jobs that require frequent face-to-face communication. Podcasting, a field so full of amateurs that the actual good ones are easy to spot, is all talk and little else. And while there is a seemingly infinite sea of podcasts available, on any and every subject under the sun, not all of them are good. Like with sex and picking out a rug, podcast taste is completely subjective, so my yuck could very well be your yum—but regardless of subject matter, style, or host, a podcast is more engaging when the voice coming out of your AirPods or whatever sounds like a real person and not like a newscaster reading from a script. Ideally, a real person that you might want to hang out with.

This isn't necessarily a requirement, but it certainly is nice to have. And of course there are exceptions to every rule; for the podcasts that are short, daily, and newsy, I suppose it's fine if the person delivering the generally horrible news is annoying, because the host's entire purpose is to be in and out quickly, without lingering, no need to say goodbye. But for the podcasts that I personally think are the best—conversational, chatty, casual, and freewheeling without feeling chaotic—I want to feel like the hosts are likable, because the personality is just as important as the content. And the podcasts that really hit, that buoy me through activities like eating a little marijuana and walking to Sephora, are the ones that feel like the Platonic ideal of a good chat between me and my smart and also beautifully stupid friends.

*Race Chaser*, a podcast hosted by former *RuPaul's Drag Race* contestants Willam and Alaska, is one such piece of work. It's clear that the two are friends, or at least friendly enough to convince me every week when I listen to them ramble; their conversation flows naturally and is, of course, studded with an "um" or "uh" or "like" every now and then. Either Willam and Alaska are seasoned professionals who are truly so confident in what they're saying that every filler word is used strategically and for emphasis, or they have a very good editor. What makes this podcast so good and so pleasant and easy to listen to is that they still sound like real people. And the thing that seals the deal is the careful and natural deployment of these filler phrases, leaving me to wonder if the hundred other "likes," "erms," and Alaska's "eeeeuuuunnghhhhh" vocal fry were left on the cutting-room floor.

Surely podcasters, forced to listen to the sounds of their own voices over and over again until they become essentially white noise, are ruthless with their editing process, slicing and dicing until the end result is legible to a wide audience. Bobby Finger is both a very good friend and the host of *Who? Weekly*, a podcast that details the comings and goings of D-list celebrities who are, in their parlance, "whos": *Love Island USA* competitors, or mid-tier influencers, or the singer Rita Ora, all of whom are not immediately recognizable by name to a general public. (Leah Kateb, from the sixth season of *Love Island USA* is a "who," but Tom Cruise is very clearly a "them.") Bobby hosts the podcast with Lindsey Weber, one of his closest friends, and the natural rapport between Lindsey and Bobby feels very much like listening to two of your smartest and funniest friends pick apart the state of modern celebrity.

Because I naturally assume that my friends who do things like make podcasts have an entire staff at their disposal, I asked

Bobby if the editor or producer of *Who? Weekly* would be willing to speak to me for this very book. My memory of when this happened is unclear, but what I do recall is Bobby laughing uproariously and correcting me. *Who? Weekly* runs a tight ship. The person behind the laptop is either Lindsey or Bobby, depending on the week. And it turns out that there is a science to making even a regular conversation sound like an elevated version of itself.

"I'll cut all the 'ums' if I can," Bobby told me over the sound of the Pointer Sisters blasting in the background of Mugs, a weird little bar in Williamsburg. Though this may sound draconian and in direct opposition to the spirit of this book, I have to agree with Bobby. "'Ums' sound bad," he said. And while I understand that "ums" are not "bad," because it's useless to say a word is "bad," I will say that an "um" that lasts for longer than, say, one-tenth of a second is occasionally grating, especially if it is abundant in regular conversation. But a podcast is not a normal conversation—it's a product that is eventually presented to the public that is, much like this book you are reading or anything else you consume, edited in a way that makes sense for the content and its intended purpose. There's an implicit understanding between creator and consumer that the creator will do their best to present work that is tidy but not overly formal and accurately represents the impromptu, conversational nature of our typical speech.

Removing "ums" from the equation makes sense, but Bobby was emphatic when I probed further about "like." "I usually cut all the ums," he said. "I try to keep as many 'likes' as possible. I cut them so that there's not too many. I cut a 'like' that makes it sound like I'm thinking. But I don't want to necessarily cut a 'like' that's just in conversation."

Keeping the 'likes' where they can do the majority of the work—inside sentences, breaking up thoughts, injecting a casual sense of fun, ease, and familiarity into a conversation—is part of what makes *Who? Weekly* such a pleasant experience. If your job is indeed to sound like a real person with thoughts, feelings, and opinions and to convey those effectively to an audience, then for the love of god, stop rapping yourself on the knuckles every time you say a "like," an "um," or an "uh." Podcasters who favor a more conversational style should feel familiar enough to their listeners but not *too* familiar—toeing the line between appreciation and a parasocial relationship. This sort of familiarity is necessary for shows like *Who? Weekly* and *Race Chaser*, but truly less so for other, different forms of podcasts. I have no interest in knowing anything more about, say, the host of *The New York Times*'s podcast *The Daily*, because I don't need my news source to have a personality—and, frankly, I'd rather they not. But two friends shooting the shit and then editing that conversation down to essentially distill its essence is where I need it.

It's not surprising that I feel this way about this situation; I am, begrudgingly, an elder millennial, and so "like" was embedded into my brain far before my prefrontal cortex was fully developed. I've probably—definitely—said it in a job interview and still gotten the job. But I suppose it never occurred to me at any point in my life to wonder if other people thought I was stupider because of the way I talk. I do not talk out loud for a living, so this is less of a concern. But Bobby clarified a point that I assumed was already true: If he and Lindsey enter the world of adult podcasts—NPR, WNYC, *The New York Times*'s audio offerings, etc.—then all bets are off. "If we are ever on an actual, fancy radio station, people comment on our 'likes' without fail, always," he said. "I've tried to tone it down; sometimes I actively try to tone it down. Because of certain appearances. But then you realize, it doesn't really matter. Our audience doesn't care. Stuffy audiences care. And they're always old people."

Because "like" conveys insecurity and a lack of self-confidence, I assume old people attribute that to a lack of professionalism or, rather, maturity—but maybe what old people are fussy about is also something that Bobby brought up. "'Likes' bother me if it's dead air, basically. If you're listening to someone think, I don't like that, if you can see the gears turning."

"Is it because you don't think the audience should see behind the curtain?" I asked.

"Nope," he said. "Even your smartest friends say 'like.'"

For the sake of fairness, I reached out to Lindsey, also a friend, in an email that I think conveyed a sense of cheerful panic. "omg is this gonna be about how much time I spend cutting my likes and bobby's Ums from the podcast????????" she wrote back in response. (Yes, Lindsey. It is!) While her approach to editing the podcast is basically the same as Bobby's—cut out the "ums" and the "uhs," but the rest of it is okay—she did say that her particular verbal tic that bothers her to hear and also to say isn't "like" but "um," or its more sophisticated cousin "uh."

"I tend to go with 'uh.' I will kind of do more of, in my mind, a French-inspired 'uh.' For some reason, 'um' to me is very American and actually very feminine," she said. What irks both parties about "um" and "uh" is one and the same: It's dead air that no one wants to hear. "I know that both of us know that we can do better," Lindsey said. "And that's the point; that's the privilege of editing your own speech is that you can take those things out." Besides the fact that an "um" sounds ugly and, in the wrong hands, an "uh" sounds like a punch in the gut, taking those words out of conversational professional speech just tightens things up—making for a listenable and even enjoyable conversation.

"I think 'likes' are harder to edit out because they're more kind of embedded in your speech," Lindsey said. "'Um' can be replaced with silence, and a 'like' cannot be really replaced with silence."

Editing a podcast that you cohost is a nice way to save money, but it also allows for control over the final product. "There's a lot of humor in our edits that comes out when we do it," Lindsey said. "And I don't think anyone else would kind of be able to inject that. And so we do that. It's just easier, you know, if we do it ourselves." Relinquishing that control to a freelance editor runs the risk of falling prey to someone else's interpretation of what sounds "right." When success, and also money, depends on authenticity and an allegiance to your own personal brand, you might want to see it through to the end yourself. Don't let someone else take the wheel when you're the one who owns the bus.

But maybe you don't want to take the wheel and, in fact,

aren't allowed to do so. News and media properties by now all have a podcasting arm that churns out any number of shows for both hyperspecific and general audiences. Take *The Daily* or NPR's *Morning Edition*: Even though the latter is live radio intercut with produced segments, and the former is definitely scripted, both shows are serving a similar purpose for a similar audience: to deliver the news to a wide audience that respects "the news" and wants to hear it from a voice of authority. *The Daily*'s description makes a bold claim: "This is what the news should sound like. The biggest stories of our time told by the best journalists in the world." If you are to take this claim at face value, paying attention to the delivery matters just as much as what's being said. Even when the interviews, like the one I listened to about air-conditioning that aired in August 2024, are unscripted, the end result is tight, authoritative, and a little bit jaunty so as to sound self-satisfied.

*The New York Times*'s audio programming is a relatively new endeavor, so perhaps the better source to look at is NPR—a venerable media outlet that is so much the standard for (occasionally) stultifying talk radio that it has been parodied on *SNL*. One of NPR's flagship programs is *Fresh Air*, hosted by the eternally soothing and altogether pleasant Terry Gross—a woman lauded for her interview skills and, if we follow this thread, ostensibly her professionalism. Because NPR is one of the grown-up media outlets on which my good pals at *Who? Weekly* would be more aware of what they're saying, imagine my surprise at learning that one word that Gross uses, like, a lot, is "like."

In a 2012 article for *Philadelphia*, Simon Van Zuylen-Wood takes a closer look at Gross's utterances and finds that Gross, an excellent interviewer with a knack for making her subjects feel at ease, leans on "like" as one of the tools in her rhetorical toolbox. "Gross uses 'like' neither as a stammering placeholder nor as a meaningless flavoring particle," he writes. "Rather, her 'likes' are stepping stones within sentences, on which she presses her weight, pivots, and tucks into her point." For Gross, Wood writes, "like" is not quite the dysfluency we've been led to believe it to be—instead, it's deployed with tact and is a direct bid for vulnerability. When interviewing writers like the late Hilary Mantel, altogether more serious and less willing to play ball, Wood says that Gross's tendency toward "like" is less apparent, adjusting her manner for her conversational partner. "Gross, in other words, uses 'like' only when *she* feels an emotional connection," he writes.

Gross's warmth isn't quite an anomaly, as I learned when I took a peek behind the curtain with Isabella Gomez Sarmiento, a producer and reporter at NPR. Before Gomez Sarmiento pivoted to reporting, she worked as a producer on *Weekend Edition*, a show that strikes a decent balance between the ticktock cadence of traditional news radio and the more conversational, breezy nature of a podcast. "*Weekend Edition* is sort of a balance because it's still very newsy, but because it's a weekend show, there are more sort of, like, 'moments of joy,'" she said.

Perhaps we can look to these moments of joy for a sign as to where the direction of radio is headed. Gomez Sarmiento told me that even though she removed some filler words and the dead air created by "um," some stayed in. "We used to say, like, 'de-um' the guest, or do a pass to clean up and straighten out some of the language, but you also wanna leave some in. So they sound like a normal person thinking, because tone is really important," she said. It turns out that even the big dogs in what I insist on calling "radio for grown-ups" recognize the power of sounding human and understand how necessary it is to keep up with the times. "Generally, I think in radio, we're moving to a place where we want people to sound more natural on air and sound less like they're reading. The less scripted people sound, the more engaging the conversation is, and that's my opinion. But it's also just feedback we tend to get from our audiences," Gomez Sarmiento told me.

Achieving this kind of natural rapport that sounds both professional and, as Gomez Sarmiento and I repeated back to each other at various points during our conversation, like normal conversation is harder when the specter of NPR's cultural influence and legacy looms large. I imagine that even the coolest of cucumbers might feel a little nervous for a radio interview on NPR and therefore would get ahead of the nerves by doing some light prep. But the best-laid plans often fail. "I feel like that can backfire, because it makes people sound really stiff," Gomez Sarmiento said. "I think sometimes it's actually disappointing when people clearly have prewritten their answers and they sound like they're reading as opposed to just actually answering a question in real time."

Gomez Sarmiento doesn't necessarily tailor her editing specifically for each show that she works on, but it is true that the quicker, newsier hits get the tighter edit while the longer and more conversational interviews—and those "moments of joy"—get a little more room to breathe. Moving toward a more casual and natural-sounding product, even for reporting the news, is progress, and the change is coming from within. "I think the more you sound like yourself, the better," Gomez Sarmiento said. "And you shouldn't feel pressured to sound a specific way." It's useful life advice, to be sure, that we could all stand to take. If we look at it as a way of, say, changing the state of the profession, then this is helpful information to have—as someone looking to move toward podcasting or radio as a profession or, more importantly, for the audio editors hired to turn chatter into commentary without sacrificing any of the humanity contained within.

A quick stroll through the subreddit dedicated to podcasting reveals insight from freelance editors, many of whom shared tips, tricks, and gripes around the editing process and how best to serve their clients. Of course, this is obvious—if you want to support yourself as a freelance audio editor working on podcasts, flexibility is your friend. As I learned from a tiresome ex who worshiped the work of renowned film editor Walter Murch, film editing is a skill set that allows for a small bit of artistry—there's a style that's recognizable in the product, even if the methodology is the same across the board. The best edit for a podcast depends, then, on the desired end result: If your intention is to sound like the BBC, you'll get a very different edit than your neighbor whose Magic: The Gathering podcast is a freewheeling and chaotic conversation about mana and how best to acquire it. A podcast wants the edit that shows at least some amount of care and consideration taken on the editor's behalf, tailoring their editing for their intended audience.

The aforementioned subreddit, r/podcasting, led me to Andy Rinaldi, an audio engineer and owner of a small private recording studio in Philadelphia. "I wasn't aware that my Reddit comments received this level of scrutiny," he wrote in an email responding to my panicked request for an audience. (To be clear, most Reddit comments don't require and should not receive any more scrutiny than a passing glance, but I was moved by how cogent, intelligent, and insightful the answers were, and so here we are.)

Rinaldi works in music composition for TV, film, and advertising and stumbled into podcast editing because it was well within his purview and very needed. "I started offering it as a service, and it got to the point where I had to take the rate sheets off my website because I would get too many calls," he told me over the phone during a rollicking and wide-ranging conversation that was interrupted only once by Rinaldi fulfilling the requests of his wife, who was self-isolating in their bedroom, nursing a case of COVID. "It's cool," he said. "I just basically get to listen to podcasts for half my day and, like, just cut them apart and shape them into what they should be."

The "should" of it all is dependent, of course, on the intended audience and desired effect—do you want your listeners to feel like they got a lot of information in very little time, or would you rather the experience of listening to two strangers talk in your earbuds as you scrub the toilet feel more like eavesdropping on a conversation between two smart people at a bar? Some of Rinaldi's clients require a "high and tight" edit or the "corporate cut"—no dead air, just sentences strung together with more sentences; efficiency at its best.

"Have you ever seen those YouTube videos where it's like they're not breathing, they're just talking, and the edit is, like, so fast, and everything's so close together? It doesn't sound natural, but it's not meant to sound natural. It's meant to cram as much information into a small amount of time as possible," he said. This approach has its place, though it's difficult to find an example that doesn't exist in a very corporate and therefore "professional" workplace. But for other, more conversational podcasts, where the content is just as important as how it's being said, Rinaldi favors a relaxed approach that allows the personalities of the hosts themselves to shine. He won't cut a stutter, nor will he edit out the labored breathing of a host who, over the course of the podcast, got progressively more drunk and fancy free—both are traits that are essential to the individual's person or personality. (The same argument does not hold for farts, in case you were wondering, like for one of Rinaldi's clients who audibly and frequently tooted on air. Arguably, such a distinctive calling card could be an inherent part of your personality, but, please, perhaps you should seek medical help.)

As we are all special snowflakes, it seems like it might be difficult for essentially a stranger to figure out what you actually sound like and to make the correct judgment call about what to keep and what to cut. Rinaldi cuts filler words, false starts, and the interminable silence of people thinking in real time, but doesn't get too surgical in his approach—the goal, after all, is to make the client happy with the result, and I can't imagine anyone would be pleased with a recording where they sound like an uncanny valley version of themselves. Steve Campagna, a recording engineer, agrees.

If saying "like" is an intrinsic part of someone's speech pattern in a recognizable way, then the word stays where it belongs. If someone really and truly says "like" so much that it feels like a compulsion, even if the purpose the word serves is useful to the speaker, then Campagna echoes the sentiments of his peers: "I would try to trim as many as possible," he said. "But if that's part of their natural speech, I would leave that in. So it doesn't sound like a completely different person."

**Chapter 7**

# Like . . . !

Like everything else in this life that is good but occasionally very bad, it is TikTok's fault for making me aware of Ice Spice, a twenty-five-year-old drill rapper from the Bronx with a shock of bright orange hair and an attitude that's less stank and more "I am who I am, so if you're bothered, don't bother me." The rapper, whose given name is Isis Gaston, is a true child of this millennium. Born on January 1, 2000, she's a Gen Z baby through and through, and so the internet is a familiar place. It is not surprising, then, that she made her initial mark during the height of the pandemic, when TikTok felt like a strange lifeline to the rest of the world, by participating in one of the interminable, flash-in-the-pan dance challenges that you see once, then roughly two hundred more times, and then never again. (The Buss It Challenge, which is what Ice Spice went viral for, involved some impressive editing and gave people the opportunity to tart it up for a club that no one was really at, from the safety of their own homes.)

During the summer of 2022, Ice Spice's music was everywhere—on TikTok, blasting out of car windows, and likely in bars and/or clubs that open for business roughly when I am crawling into bed to watch television. Her first single, "Munch (Feelin' U)," premiered on WorldStarHipHop—a purveyor of new music as well as some of the wildest fight and prank videos you will ever see—and upon first and then every subsequent viewing, I was mesmerized. The audacity of this child, literally born the year I graduated high school, invigorated me. "Munch (Feelin' U)" is peppered with hyperspecific regional slang from the Bronx drill rap scene—illegible enough to the general public that Complex published a guide to modern New York drill slang in October of that year, so as to better help your cousin Alicia in Tempe understand what a "munch" is without having to get on a plane and see for herself.

Part of what makes Ice Spice's entire deal so mesmerizing is the slang—her deft use of language in new and exciting ways. "Munch," for example, is basically what it sounds like, and if you have a filthy mind and can understand context clues, you should be able to figure out what it means. The song came about not quite as an afterthought but more of a personal challenge to make a song as fast as possible, with none of the hemming and hawing one assumes accompanies a hit. "I was just like, 'How can I describe a desperate man that wants to eat it all the time?' And I was just like, 'Munch. He's a munch,'" she told Jeff Ihaza in *Rolling Stone*.

Further clarification on the new definition of "munch" can be found in one of the internet's most entertaining sources for slang—Urban Dictionary, a user-compiled glossary that provides something close to a real-time view of how teenagers are using their words and how fast it's all changing. The entry for "munch" is 116 pages long, each definition its own interpretation, occasionally colored with hyperspecific references that read like little inside jokes left on the internet for their targets to one day find. (This is true of almost all the entries, and a very nice way to kill some time is to search your name to see what happens. The top entry for "Megan" contains a nugget of truth that really resonated with me: "Once a Megan trusts you, do NOT betray that trust because she isn't going to wait for karma to get you, she'll just get you herself... She isn't scared of anybody and the only thing she truly fears is losing somebody she loves." Thank you, SelithiaLove, the 2017 author of this definition, for seeing me so clearly.)

A munch isn't just a man you keep around for oral fulfillment; he's a bit of a sad character—he's obsessed with the target of his desire, and his love, unrequited. No one wants to be a munch, even if a munch's primary activity is something he enjoys doing and you enjoy receiving, because a munch's whole deal is that he'll only ever get as far as third base. "Munch" isn't a word that I personally use very often, perhaps because I don't have one in my life, but the meaning has irrevocably changed. And that's fine!

"Munch (Feelin' U)" is the lead single from Ice Spice's debut EP, *Like..?*, a title sure to irritate the very same grammarians that bristle at vocal fry. And honestly, that might be part of the point. In a review at *Pitchfork*, Heven Haile picks up on the clever subversion. "For Ice Spice, 'like' is less of a filler and more of a mouth gag," she writes. "Like, shut up when she's speaking," but also shut up when she's not. It's this attitude that's part of the gag. "Like," with its generally negative associations with empty-headed teenage girls with voices as creaky as screen doors, becomes a cheeky provocation. At the risk of making assumptions, we spend a lot of time making fun of how teen girls talk, only to find ourselves with our metaphorical dicks in our hands when we end up adopting their innovations for ourselves.

I find Ice Spice's general vibe to be aspirational, though I recognize that the vast chasm in our ages generally allows her to get away with a little more than I ever could. My old brain is not nimble enough to identify and then name the kind of man whose utility is just giving head; I also wouldn't ever find myself in coochie cutters and a tube top shaking my ass in and around a group of my peers. (Never say never!) However, I'd like to take the philosophy of such an act into my daily life. I do like Ice Spice's music, even though it occasionally makes me feel old and dusty—and I remain enamored with her joie de vivre, which is perhaps the most relatable thing about her to me. And her skillful deployment of "like" in this particular context—and the potential for what can be—is worthy of a closer look.

At this point, we have well established that women, but especially young women, are at the forefront of linguistic change. As of this book's writing, Ice Spice is of the exact demographic leading the charge. And there's a strong case to be made here for this lesser-known usage, which, to my mind, can take off.

Unfortunately, the next story I'm about to relay tears a giant hole in the tenuous scrim of my credibility. Muffy Siegel is an accomplished ventriloquist, a professor at the University of Pennsylvania, and the author of a very useful study about "like" and teenage girls—one of many that I've read exhaustively over the course of this writing. On a phone call, she acknowledged the large elephant in the room: I'm not a linguist, just someone who talks before they think and then kicks themselves for it later.

Emboldened by Dr. Siegel's brevity and encouraged by her support, I pressed on, presenting a theory I made up that, unsurprisingly, doesn't pan out: Can we make a case for "Like..." to be a full sentence?

"I had noticed quite a while ago, the expansion of 'like' before a whole sentence and having it applied to the whole sentence," she said. But regarding my position, which I was prepared to defend to the death, she was clear. "So because of the ellipsis, it doesn't count as a one-word sentence, right? It's elliptical... you're supposed to fill in the rest."

As we all remember from high school, a sentence must have a subject and a verb; by these very exacting and immovable qualifications, "Like..." doesn't fly. But I assumed that it *could* function as the only word in a sentence, in part because of how useful it is. "Like...," specifically, is my preferred delivery of this word, and with all apologies to every English teacher I've ever had, fuck me for thinking that this sort of thing can be subject to change! Ice Spice's use of the (grammatically incorrect but who's counting?) sentence "Like..?" *should* position this use to recur with some frequency, not just because she's of the right age and milieu to influence culture, but because of how useful it is. Betting on potential will often result in heartbreak, but what kind of life will you live if you don't take a risk?

Using "like" as a full sentence, as Ice Spice has done, isn't nearly as common as the other myriad ways the word is used—or abused, depending on who you ask. When "like" comprises the entirety of a sentence, the meaning feels pretty clear. There's very little up for interpretation. It's a retort, an entreaty for peace, an exhortation. The options for punctuating the end of a sentence are fairly limited and also obvious—there are just three, and you know exactly what they are. But when "like" is the only word in your sentence, it's a real hoot to see what each one can do in a situation where almost everything can be left to interpretation.

Here are some pertinent examples.

"Like . . . ?" is an appropriate response in any situation where you're looking for emotional validation after describing an interpersonal situation where you were clearly wronged:

*"Elizabeth asked me to bring Alfredo's juice box and to finish his trigonometry homework while I was sitting down to pee for the first time in, like, three days. Like . . . ?"*

"Like!" communicates surprise and indignation—a neat and tidy way of reacting to a situation where gall is involved:

*"Alfredo failed algebra, and now Andrea's doing his trigonometry homework. Like! Are we serious? Are we kidding me?"*

"Like . . ." is a beautiful, open-ended statement that can easily slot into any lull in a conversation; if we're being technical, though, it's a sentence fragment. In proper, regular, spoken English, a sentence has a noun, a verb, a subject, and an end. "The cat asked Jessica if she *really* wanted osso buco for dinner" is a full sentence. "The cat asked Jessica if she really wanted osso buco for dinner . . ." technically is not. The ellipsis here makes this statement open-ended, as if the narrative that begins here could go on indefinitely. In the first scenario, the cat knows that Jessica definitely wants osso buco for dinner but figured she'd ask first, just to check before she runs to the butcher for veal shanks. And while technically, the second sentence isn't a sentence because of the open ellipsis at the end, it's pretty clear what's happening here. The cat understands that she'll have to eventually make osso buco today, but because Jessica's had it at least three times this past month, she's wondering if there's space for a different dinner option—something lighter and slightly more seasonally appropriate for early fall, like a nice amatriciana or something of the sort. There's space here for Jessica to take an alternate route; the ellipsis allows her to really consider the assumption made here by her magical cat. What does it say about her self-perception as a low-maintenance individual that the beleaguered cat chef, standing at the kitchen sink with her paws on her hips, is basically asking for permission to make something simple?

In casual conversation, a sentence that ends in an ellipsis, like in the tale of Jessica, the osso buco, and the cat, doesn't even register as grammatically incorrect because of the context. But a sentence like this irritates my computer's built-in pedant, saying in a quiet, firm tone that I had better finish my thought—or else. But if language and the way we use it change every day and so quickly that we don't even know what's happening when they do, then it stands to reason that a sentence like "Like..." could one day be generally accepted as grammatically correct, even though it currently isn't.

And unlike the two previous examples that I've just cited, I noticed that I say "Like..." on its own most frequently in communication that lives in the liminal space between written and verbal speech: text messages, Slack, or any other platform that exists as a piss-poor stand-in for face-to-face communication.

Text-based messaging appears to be my preferred method of communication, though I would argue that frequency of use doesn't correlate with preference. Personally, I'm lazy, I like my alone time, and, to paraphrase the words of Kim Cattrall, I don't want to be anywhere for even an hour if I am not having a nice time. Despite how terrible this medium is for serious or meaningful conversations, sometimes it's the easiest way. And because texting is essentially like speaking with your thumbs into your phone, it makes sense that the way we speak and the way we text aren't too different.

Just like there are arbitrary rules for how to speak clearly, similar rules apply for writing. Style books of the *Eats, Shoots & Leaves* variety are useful resources and make decent gifts for college graduates. Even though it feels uncomfortable and therefore sort of bad to hear that the way you write or speak could use some improvement, as with anything in life, the way the message is delivered matters just as much as the message itself. This is why I suggest that anyone who wants to think about how their communication could be clearer (this is everyone on Earth, I assume) read a style guide that is at least written with

## Megan C. Reynolds

an eye toward the layperson who wants to know how to improve their emails or whatever without feeling chastised.

Benjamin Dreyer's book *Dreyer's English: An Utterly Correct Guide to Clarity and Style* is precisely that bitch. In 320 sprightly pages, Dreyer issues advice and general rules to follow, in a manner that probably won't make anyone feel bad about themselves after reading it. In this particular space, this is a gift. A section on dangling modifiers finally cleared up any confusion I'd been harboring about what exactly a dangling modifier even is. (The section on the subjunctive mood is the only thing I've read that has actually made a lick of sense, and for this, I am grateful.) In fact, Dreyer is most prescriptive—and hardly so—in the chapter about fiction, where he urges for consistency, clarity, and verisimilitude. The rules are different but also pretty much the same—if you're striving for clarity in your quiet novel about the Great Depression or an email asking for a month off so you can train to climb Mt. Everest, then just be careful and considerate with what you're saying and how you're saying it.

A brief section about sentence fragments uses the opening paragraph of Charles Dickens's *Bleak House* to illustrate the point that sometimes fragments are okay, but in the same breath notes that plenty of modern fiction employs such a thing "to establish a sort of hairy, sweaty, unbathed masculine narrative voice," which is a devastating and accurate burn that also happens to be true. However, Dreyer's insistence that, if used correctly and sparingly, a sentence fragment can be of some stylistic use buoyed my confidence enough to stand behind my feelings about "like" and how it can exist as a fragment itself, even if it is grammatically incorrect. Now that I've framed it as a stylistic choice rather than a choice born out of ignorance or something approaching stupidity, I feel a greater sense of peace. My way isn't the highway (yet), but it's not entirely wrong, either. "Like" can be a full sentence, even if it *is* a fragment, and I will gladly take up this fight until I am dead in the ground.

Blessedly, there is further anecdotal evidence that, if you squint, supports my claim. In *Because Internet: Understanding The New Rules of Language*, self-described internet linguist Gretchen McCulloch points to the utility of the ellipsis (the "dot-dot-dot," in her parlance), especially when it comes to "chat"—the text-based communication that bridges the gap between speaking and writing.

For her purposes, McCulloch slots the general public into three different categories, based on their familiarity with the internet and its sustained presence in their lives—not by age or generation but by how they first encountered the internet as a social tool. "Old Internet People" met strangers (and interacted with real-life friends) on Usenet, a sprawling online forum whose modern analogue is Reddit. (Though McCulloch is careful not to mention age, it's clear that an Old Internet Person is resolutely Gen X.) "Semi-Internet People" encountered the internet's social possibilities through messenger-based chat, like MSN Messenger and AIM, may she rest in peace. Again, while age is nothing but a number, Semi-Internet People by now are middle-aged—the tail end of Gen X and the oldest millennials understand the internet's potential just enough to fear it a little. "Full Internet People" are your average monstera-leaf-loving millennials—young enough for *Lizzie McGuire* to be a foundational text—who first encountered the internet in its capacity as an actual social network, via Facebook or Twitter. (MySpace is nowhere in McCulloch's taxonomy, but if you can remember who was in your Top 8, you're probably old enough to be getting your first doctor-mandated colonoscopy.)

The final group, of which I'd say Ice Spice is a member, are truly what marketing executives call "digital natives"—they live, breathe, and create the internet in a way that's both exhilarating and exhausting. Their first interactions were on platforms like Snapchat, Vine, Instagram, and TikTok, all platforms tailor-made for the hopes and dreams of millions of people trying to make it big by being themselves—just like Ice Spice did when she rode the plentiful waves of mid-pandemic TikTok, when seemingly everyone was chasing or achieving virality. The difference here is that Ice Spice parlayed her proverbial fifteen minutes into an actual career, harnessing the power of the internet and her fans to make some linguistic change.

According to McCulloch, the internet is essentially a large gathering of many smaller groups, each with their own vocabularies, glossaries, and social cues, most of which are (intentionally) illegible to people outside of that particular fold. And it's the languages within these groups—"in-group language," or shared ways of speaking that are particular to the group in question—that have a profound impact and influence on the way we speak as we go from youth to adulthood.

Early adolescence is when your language influences shift from your parents to your peer group, tracking neatly with the general teen distaste for anything your parents hold dear and may have championed as "correct." Even if what your parents believe in is in line with your own beliefs, aligning yourself with their way of thinking is anathema. What McCulloch and almost every other book, research paper, blog post, article, and interview I've read reiterate is this: Gender and age are the two biggest influences in how language changes. And, yes, the fact that women are the leaders of this change is often glossed over, but it is an irrefutable fact. Use this as a talking point on a horrible date with a grammar corrector, or perhaps in a job interview, or really any scenario where you want to impress your intelligence upon your target while also gently debasing them.

(I urge you to sit with this information for a second and think of all the marvelous ways you can apply it in your everyday life. Never would I ever advocate for being a know-it-all, but it's certainly nice to dabble every now and again—good for gut health and also your own mental acuity. So the next time someone feels compelled to tell you that you're saying "like" too much, just tell them that the reason you and the rest of the world say this at all is because of the collective power of teenage girls. See if that resonates. If it doesn't, leave!)

But, really, language change spreads so quickly because of what sociologist Mark Granovetter calls "weak ties" and "strong ties." In his groundbreaking 1973 paper, "The Strength of Weak Ties," Granovetter presents a theory of social connection. He surveyed a group of 282 men to see how they got their jobs and found that casual acquaintances and loose connections—the aforementioned weak ties—were instrumental in helping these men find employment. Our strong ties—family and friends whom you see and talk to frequently—were less helpful in this regard. While Granovetter's finding might seem obvious now, it was revelatory information in 1973, and this theory applies across a wide variety of academic fields, including psychology, economics, business, and linguistics. Your weak ties and your strong ties are instrumental in how language change spreads. Counterintuitively, we learn new forms of language and speaking via the weak ties—social groups that you follow online that you aren't actually a part of, or as a result of the parasocial relationship you've formed with a mid-tier influencer on TikTok—but we spread these new forms via the strong ties that are already established.

Teenagers are already highly susceptible to new ways of speaking and thinking and are eager to glom on to actions that feel rebellious. A teenage girl with unfettered access to the internet is essentially an explorer setting sail on uncharted waters and eventually returning with a vast trove of new knowledge and ways of being in this world. This is a very simplistic explanation for how language changes, works, and evolves, but for our purposes, simplicity is better. And McCulloch's argument is that the internet is an essential part of this process because it's a breeding ground for weak ties and therefore helps new forms of language spread much, much faster.

Even though I know that "Like . . ." is not a full sentence, part of me thinks it should be, if only because of how often it shows up in my written communication with friends. Based on its frequency of use with not only myself but also my friends, maybe it already is. The difference between "Like . . . ?" and "Like!" feels pretty clear, and that clarity is due to the punctuation mark that closes the ellipsis. But "Like . . ." leaves room for interpretation and lets a little emotion slide in, just in case. Cramming *that* kind of "like" into my texts and chats gives the mundane some dramatic flair by making up for the lack of visual context that accompanies a riotous conversation between friends in person.

If my friend Julianne sends me a link to a pair of ugly mesh Mary Janes that are mostly hideous because of the unflattering strap placement across the vamp and follows that message with "Like . . . ," I have a pretty good idea of what she's trying to say! First, this is a skill that comes from knowing someone for a long time, working under them for a few years, and then emerging from that toxic work environment with a friendship miraculously intact. Second, between existential conversations about productivity, inner saboteurs, and whether we should go to that thing we were both invited to, fashion is a primary topic of conversation. This context, which is only known to the two of us, informs the rest of this conversation, as well as the initial "like" entreaty.

The shoe in question is hideous; perhaps Bella Hadid wore it once, and now I see a knockoff sitting in the Amazon cart I share with my youngest sister. The original shoe, an Alaïa mesh Mary Jane, retails for $890 and therefore is far too expensive for Julianne or myself to buy, would either one of us want to wear such a thing—a fact that I clocked immediately when clocking the shoe itself. And furthermore, the shoe is a throwback to the early 2000s, and now that the teenagers are wearing it and many other horrid mistakes, like handkerchief-hem maxi skirts and Capri pants, the shoe's mere existence makes us feel, on some level, very tired. That one "like," typed into a chat box while we both toil away at our respective computers, says more with less. It's an open-ended question or, rather, a vessel for context and history between friends.

Using "like" at the beginning of a sentence or even just on its own, as I am trying repeatedly to do here, thanks, is actually doing similar work as the quotative use, when "be like" subs in for "say" in retelling a story or conversation. "If you think about a direct quote, like if I'm quoting something that someone said or thought or gestured, that is itself a sentence," Alexandra D'Arcy, the linguistics professor whose work on the word is the authority, told me, thus affirming a long-held belief that this entire chapter is attempting to prove in one way or another. A "like" at the start of a sentence is a way to link what came before with what's coming now and is essentially a mark of decent storytelling skills, or at least the desire to relate to another person without sounding stiff or stilted. Don't show up to the function in a ball gown when everybody else is in cargo shorts. Even if the cargo shorts offend you on a cellular level, please read the room.

Besides, an authoritative "like" at the start of a sentence is a way to take the floor—an announcement of sorts that you're about to do or say something worth paying attention to, like when Ice Spice's *Like..?* EP burst on the scene. And while there's definitely an argument to be made that stretching the meaning of a word that has already been pulled and stretched like hot taffy is pointless, the answer to that is simple: "Like . . . ?"

**Conclusion**

# Like, What's Next?

Over the course of my writing this book, every woman I spoke to had a story about how someone at some point made her feel badly for saying "like." Usually the critic was a man, and more often than not, it was her father or some other paternal figure, who felt it their personal responsibility to change the way a woman speaks—for her own good.

I count myself blessed to not be one of this number: If memory serves, my father never corrected or chastised me for how I spoke, though I imagine I did get some blowback that one time, in the midst of an argument, I called him a douchebag (an insult that he did not deserve). My mother's grammar correctives are relatively nonexistent, but she hates "cussing" and assiduously avoids using curse words. ("A-H-hole," her way of calling someone an asshole, is redundant but specific. I will remember it for the rest of my time on this earth.)

These aforementioned women, most of whom are in public-facing positions that involve podcasting or various branches of the federal government, have all told me that these comments stick. No one likes being corrected. Doing so is largely a waste of time, because even if you think you're cutting off an error at the source, there's always going to be a new generation on the sidelines, waiting to go in. Youth is a renewable resource. And every generation will bring some sort of linguistic change that they literally breathed into existence.

Making a case for the validity of "like" is making a case for progress—or for at least understanding that progress and change are not necessarily the enemy. First of all, change is inevitable, and feeling any type of way about it other than begrudging acceptance is probably a waste of time. Second, sociocultural progress is the thing that keeps language moving forward. The rules are merely guidelines, firm suggestions that you can feel free to ignore in the service of a larger progressive shift. Adhering to the rules just for the sake of doing so carries more than a whiff of hall monitor energy. This isn't policing language—it's common sense. It'd make a little *more* sense if there were something more nefarious lurking under the surface of this linguistic commotion, like if saying "like" instead of "said" when telling a story were as bad as fracking—or if language were being manipulated to undermine an underprivileged group—but most of the criticisms leveled at "like" are garden-variety misogyny. Negative reactions to new concepts are born of fear. Although teenage girls aren't inherently scary, they can be intimidating to some people because of their innate ability to make everyone around them feel deeply, pathologically uncool.

Arguably, coolness is an ineffable set of traits that, like with porn, you know when you see it. I'd also argue that in this very specific instance, all "cool" really means is "young and therefore much further away from death." Teenagers remind us of our own mortality by their mere existence; they aren't flaunting their youth so much as they are just living their lives. The difference, of course, is that in this fictitious scenario, the older people and the teenagers whose mere existence seems to have pissed them off are approaching any interaction from opposite ends of the spectrum—teenagers remain convinced on some level that they are invincible, while as people get older, that invincibility is replaced with a mortal reckoning. This vague theory doesn't apply to babies or children, for they are innocent little potatoes full of joy, and to be cynical about death in the face of a child feels like one step too far. But teenagers exist in the liminal space between childhood and adulthood, making it feel crucial for some people to intercede before their brains settle and their speech patterns are "ruined for good." "I'm not known for my speaking ability, but I did have 'like' scolded out of my vocab," my sister Tessa texted the three of us in the group chat. While Tessa's father (my stepfather, for those following along) had the best of intentions, it didn't matter—these sorts of things stick in the craw and are quite difficult to get rid of. At some point, you have to wonder— why bother?

It would be much easier to throw up your hands in defeat and give in than to dig your heels in and stay put. It's difficult but not impossible to learn a language that isn't your native tongue, for example, but people do it all the time for work, for leisure, or out of necessity. The work of learning a new language literally restructures and changes your brain, according to a study by

Dr. Xuehu Wei at the Max Planck Institute for Human Cognitive and Brain Sciences in Leipzig, Germany. Over a period of six months, Dr. Wei studied the brain scans of fifty-nine native Arabic speakers—Syrian refugees participating in a German-language intensive—to see how and if their brains changed over time. The results showed that stronger connections developed in the language sectors of both the right and the left hemispheres of the brain, but the connections between the two decreased, meaning that the left side of your brain, where "most language centers are located, loses some control over the right hemisphere to compensate for the increased networks required during the later stages of language learning. Therefore, it can be concluded that the process of learning German was demanding enough to create major alterations in brain circuitry," the study reads. Assuming (correctly) that these alterations are not specific to German, a language with words like "Lebensabschnittsgefährte," which means "domestic partner," we can infer that the human brain is indeed capable of change. New synaptic pathways are created so that your big, mushy brain can learn more stuff, make new connections, and, in general, keep things running for as long as possible. Life is arduous at times, longer than it needs to be, and can be terrifically boring. But the alternative is less than ideal. We don't know when we're going to die, but everybody does eventually. Why not try and make the most of it by expanding our linguistic possibilities instead of contracting them?

Maybe the thought that our brains are still elastic and not set in stone is the scary part. There is an admittedly large chasm between picking up conversational Swiss German in middle age and learning to love—or at least tolerate—new ways of speaking, and there's value in giving it a shot, but think of it this way: If a daily sudoku practice to stave off dementia feels like the last thing you want to do, but the march of time and the inevitable havoc it may wreak on your brain scares you, maybe don't get so tight about a woman on the radio saying "like" where *you* think it doesn't belong. If you open your mind to the world's unrelenting march forward, what's the harm in that?

I understand that although embracing the unknown might make for a happier life, putting that notion into practice can be immensely difficult. And one of the more pressing questions about anything is why: Why do I need to care? Why is this exciting? Why will whatever you're saying impact my life? All valid questions with a long-winded answer: More expansive communication fosters more expansive connection. Our speech patterns, vocabularies, and language shift over time in service of clarity, even if this may not seem evident at first. If you don't have the right words to say what you mean, then you should feel joy and excitement when new ways of self-expression are unlocked. In fact, the idea that we can actually stretch the rules to the breaking point and mold the language that exists into something else that is ultimately more nuanced and therefore clearer is exciting. How thrilling to think that there are words out there, adrift in the ether, that could get second or third lives with new meanings that come because of people expressing themselves in new and different ways.

What I find far more exciting than change is potential. At the risk of sounding like a self-help Instagram Reel, all anyone wants (and deserves) in this short life is to feel seen and to be heard. And sometimes the language for that doesn't yet exist or the current inventory of words and their meanings feels stale and staid. Why not try something new and see what sticks?

The new ways of speaking are the domain of the young, and once their words (like "like") have infiltrated the mainstream, the word's cool evaporates—and so does the general fuss over its existence in the first place. (Everything is temporary!) To see this in theory, let's turn to "bae," a word that is by now commonplace enough to warrant little notice. "Bae" is a mid-2010s slang word and term of endearment that purportedly stands for "before anyone else" and has been in use since roughly 2013. As is almost standard at this point, "bae" gained a foothold on Black Twitter, and eventually its ubiquity lunged it into the mainstream, where it reached the next step in its evolution as the subject of an occasional grumpy or whiny op-ed. "What the hell is up with 'bae'?" *Esquire* asked in 2014. "Is it really that much harder to say 'babe' than 'bae'? Plus, are descriptions such as actual proper names and the words 'best friend,' 'lover,' 'irreplaceable,' 'incomparable,' etc., no longer good enough?" Even though I suspect that this article was published not out of a desire to answer this question, but rather to appease Google's search algorithm by publishing content aimed at answering a question that many people were googling, I think the rhetorical questions posed here are worth a closer look.

It's not that it's so difficult to say "babe" that language evolved to completely drop the second *b*—we just made space in the lexicon of pet names to include a variation on a theme.

And the other descriptive words one might use for their bae, as provided by *Esquire,* are, unfortunately, not sufficient to explain the wide variety of nuance present in interpersonal relationships. What pet names like "bae," "baby," "cookie," "babe," "honey," "sweetie," "dumpling," "peanut," or "Mr. Handsome" communicate is not just affection but the *kind* of affection you feel toward the object of your desire. Multiple words for the same concept—in this case, a romantic partner—usually suggest that the concept in question is complicated or otherwise significant. If you really do care about someone and want to be specific in how you communicate the breadth of your affection when talking to other people, then having a lot of options allows you to speak with specificity and freedom. This aspect of English is a feature, not a bug. For words like "bae," complete mainstream saturation generally occurs when brands start using the word to sell stuff. If you see a tweet from Cheez-Its proclaiming that its new Jalapeño Gouda Cheddar XXXtra Crisp Crackerdoodles are #bae, then the word's credibility evaporates, never to be seen again. "Bae" then becomes a word you see on a cheeky Hallmark card, your grandmother asks you what it means at Thanksgiving cocktail hour, the world keeps spinning, and life soldiers on. Everyone's learned a little something and is no worse for the wear.

Words transform and change through misuse, as we effectively weed out the ways that don't work in favor of something that does. English absorbs words from different languages and cultures all the time and introduces them into our day-to-day. Certainly, people get angry about this, but that's true of everything that's fun and ultimately beneficial. If you don't make a few people mad along the way, then what's the point of living at all? What's so truly magical about language is its flexibility. In their book *Origins of the Specious: Myths and Misconceptions of the English Language*, Patricia T. O'Conner and Stewart Kellerman write, "Like it or not, correctness is determined by common practice, even when a new usage collides with an old established rule." This sentiment is echoed in the journey of "like," but if you'd like a concrete example, let's look at one of the subtle differences between American English and British English that likely grates parties on both sides of the pond. This difference goes beyond the fact that in the United States, the sleeveless fleece zip-up garment favored by tech entrepreneurs and boomer dads is known as a "vest," while the British refer to the same garment as the very continental "gilet."

The wide-ranging differences here are enough to fill another book that many other people have written, but for our exercises, let's look at collective nouns. In American English, we treat collective nouns as singular entities, and in British English, they can be either-or. This may seem like a minor difference, but when you hear it in practice, you will never be able to shake how foreign it sounds. "The band is waiting for Mrs. Thistlethwaite" is correct in Peoria, Illinois. If this scenario took place in Hartlepool, England, you might hear the vicar whisper to the butcher, "The band are waiting for Mrs Thistlethwaite," and to your American ears, that sounds batty, awkward, and very wrong. What's so beautiful about this example is that, after a few passes over the "right" way and the "wrong" way to say it, you eventually reach the conclusion that none of this truly matters.

Perhaps I've been immersed in this world and am therefore now paying closer attention to how people are speaking, but when a grammar "rule" cuts through much of my interior monologue and makes me question its validity, then I have to wonder how useful that rule actually is. Splitting an infinitive, an activity that I perform with reckless abandon, isn't life-or-death.

"I decided to carefully address my feelings about Marjorie's new hairless cat, Reginald, because Marjorie can be quite sensitive" contains a split infinitive that, until recently, did not register. The correct version of this story, "I decided to address carefully my feelings about Marjorie's new hairless cat, Reginald," conveys the same meaning but is smugly correct in a way that, again, deserves a wedgie at the minimum. "To this day, many thoughtful, educated people will turn a sentence inside out to avoid a split infinitive," O'Conner and Kellerman write. While I salute them in their efforts to preserve a version of the language that is already extinct, I can't support it. The "wrong" version sounds right to me, and as I have told myself for the majority of my life, if something sounds right, then there's a decent chance that it probably is.

(The reason for any hubbub over this rule and others is simple. According to O'Conner and Kellerman, when two new editions of the *Oxford English Dictionary*—one American and one British—were published in 1998, a press release insisted that it was okay to split infinitives, creating a very unnecessary amount of public hand-wringing over something that, again, is helpful rather than harmful.)

Another rule, against starting a sentence with a conjunction, may have been drilled into our heads as wrong by English teachers who were sick of reading student papers where every other sentence started with "and." These rules are arbitrary, occasionally born from personal grudges, and are meant to be broken if doing so makes it easier to feel heard. Language and grammatical changes that provide clarity and ease communication so that it's effective and not just a dick-waving contest over who knows more SAT words is overall a net positive. Life is hard enough! "My own feeling is that it's better to be understood than to be correct, especially when intelligent people can't agree on what is correct," O'Conner and Kellerman write.

When it comes to conjunctions, it's worth remembering that when "like" was first used as a conjunction, it caused a minor outrage. In 1954 Winston Cigarettes came out with a new slogan: "Winston tastes good like a cigarette should." Sit with that sentence. Read it out loud. See how nicely it rolls off the tongue. It's a beautiful advertising slogan, succinct and to the point, and memorable because of the assonance in "good" and "should," separated by a "like" that, as many hollered about at the time, was grammatically incorrect and didn't belong there at all. Technically, the sentence should read "Winston cigarettes taste good, as a cigarette should," but there's nothing snappy about that, and the sibilance of "as," jammed in the middle there, gunks up the works. In poetics, how language sounds is as important as how it reads on the page; the *s* at the end of "as" is a voiced consonant and lacks the sexy, slippery, and suggestive sibilance of the string of adjectives you just read in this sentence. The *s* sounds like the buzz of a mosquito or a swarm of bees. It is not a hospitable sound, and if you rush through that sentence, the "as" sort of gets swallowed up. But the sound of "like" contains a much more pleasing and dynamic sound—a voiceless plosive, sort of like a sharp exhale. Block your soft palate with the back of your tongue, then let it go—or just say "like" out loud over and over again, until that sharpness registers. To my ears—and perhaps to the ears of many of R. J. Reynolds's target audience, which at that time was basically everyone—the grammatically correct version of the slogan is a stick in the mud, a pinch-nosed pedant pushing his glasses up his nose with satisfaction as he corrects you.

The slogan's debut stirred up a bit of controversy (all the better for cigarettes, horrible things, god bless them), but most notably with the most trusted man in America, Walter Cronkite. As a young newscaster at CBS in 1954, Cronkite was tasked with reading an on-air advertisement for Winston and found himself simply incapable of violating the sacred rules of grammar. When he read the ad, he said "as" and not "like" and caused a lot of bother. "I can't do an ungrammatical thing like that," he said to Don Carleton in a 1999 interview, much to the chagrin of the advertising executives in the control room. Furthermore, the ad required Cronkite, a nonsmoker, to pick up a cigarette and inhale. This, too, he refused, though I would argue that this refusal carries a little more water. Cronkite's reaction to this transgression was because of its newness, but also because of how "wrong" it sounded to him. But as O'Conner and Kellerman tell it, using "like" as a conjunction dates to Chaucerian times, and we carried on using it in this way for centuries, and it didn't become an issue until the nineteenth century. "The objection was apparently that too many people were likely to do it," O'Conner and Kellerman write. "In other words, it had become too common for the language snobs of the day."

Upholding the mythical standards of language and how it should be used is just another way of clinging to a version of the past that feels comfortable instead of leaning in to change, even for a little bit, and is a waste of energy. Solve world hunger! Cultivate a hobby. There are roughly 127 other things to do with your time, so you might as well make the most of it. Leave this particular bugbear in the past, where it belongs.

For all the hubbub around how words and therefore meaning change over time, it's crucial to remember that in this game, the people have more control than they realize. "In the end, it's not the grammarians and usage experts who decide what's right. It's you—the people who actually use the language day in and day out," O'Conner and Kellerman write. And nowhere is *that* rule, which is the only one worth really paying attention to, more evident than in the case of "literally," another "like"-adjacent word that has, over the years, developed many different meanings and usages that grate just as much as "like" has in the past. O'Conner herself is personally wedded to "literally's" meaning staying static, but she does hold space for other interpretations.

## Megan C. Reynolds

Records show that in the late 1700s, "literally" was being used much in the same way that we use it in modern times—to emphasize or elaborate on figurative or metaphorical statements. For example: If I sidebar with one of my many sisters about how I am literally going to scream if one of our *other* sisters continues to ask for the streaming platform logins that she definitely already has in her email, chances are that I'm not actually screaming. (I don't like loud noises, and screaming would scare the cat.) But throwing that "literally" into this sentence merely emphasizes my point—and I suppose there's a chance that I actually *would* scream should the mood strike, but it's pretty low. Another, more dramatic example highlights how I'd actually use this word (and is a paraphrase of a sentence that I've likely said in some capacity over the course of writing this book):

*"We literally cannot keep saying that 'like' is a bad word, because if I have to entertain this line of reasoning for one more minute, I will literally fake my own death and fuck off to Bali with the cat."*

Here are some reasonable assumptions: The speaker—me, if you're following—would like the world at large to relax. If that's not possible in a way that I find suitable, I probably won't fake my own death, in part because it seems like a *lot* of work, but I will do whatever feels like a realistic equivalent. Taking to the sofa with a grip of edibles and starting *The Real Housewives of Beverly Hills* from the very beginning, with my phone on Do Not Disturb and the cat rotting in silence next to me, produces the same result as a successful faked death and lacks any of the onerous administrative work I imagine faking your own death requires. Because you're a smart cookie, you were able to infer this from context clues. However, without the "literally," this sentence would lack the punch I desire. It's a rhetorical flourish that underscores how I would like everyone listening to understand the depths of my desire to vacate my life—temporarily, of course. How lovely it is that we have a word that allows us to do this.

Other uses of "literally" are biding their time in the wings. If we can use "literally" to add a hyperbolic flair to a story, then maybe the word can also stand in for assent. I'm not a mage, nor am I a psychic, but if we want to look toward the future of language like "like" and "literally"—unconventional and innovative uses of words, pioneered by young women who are routinely mocked for it—then there's a lot of excitement on the horizon. And if I were to pick a leader for this movement, I would turn to Leah Kateb, a contestant on the sixth season of *Love Island USA*, and I would pay very close attention to what she says and how she says it. In fact, the entire cast of *Love Island USA* is an excellent case study—young and hot TV people striving for fame, human connection, or some combination of both.

On *Love Island USA*, Leah, a twenty-five-year-old from Calabasas with a fair amount of skillfully executed elective surgery, is a compelling figure—funny and self-aware enough to recognize that she needs a man who, in her words, should make her feel like she could use a stint in the psych ward. She finds this psych ward feeling—one that I recognize as maybe a symptom of attachment issues—in Rob Rausch, a twenty-six-year-old social media snake wrangler from Alabama who looks like he walked out of a vintage Abercrombie ad and dresses and occasionally acts like a fuckboy from Williamsburg who might give you gonorrhea. (None of those is a negative, and in fact, when these are all combined, they create a powerful force that is difficult to resist.) Both parties are attractive, and their flames burn brighter in the company of each other. This couple is compelling enough to watch all thirty-seven episodes of a *Love Island USA* season, but that distracts from my point. Leah and Rob are a short-lived couple that, if the show were anything like reality, would probably still be fucking every now and again and not making it a very big deal. (I find it alarming that I find communion with this woman, as I am nearly twice her age and should reasonably know better by now, but the heart wants what it wants. I recognize Leah's patterns, and I pray she finds peace.)

After Leah was voted off *Love Island USA* by the public, she went straight to the Los Angeles studio of the podcast *Call Her Daddy*, hosted by Alex Cooper, who *Rolling Stone* called Gen Z's Barbara Walters. (The comparison is apt, but Cooper's evolution really follows that of another wildly popular radio host with a controversial past—the king of all media himself, Howard Stern.) *Call Her Daddy* started in 2018, with Cooper and former cohost (and friend) Sofia Franklyn hopping on a mic and talking to each other in a way that recalls the women of Ariel Levy's 2005 book *Female Chauvinist Pigs: Women and the Rise of Raunch Culture*—speaking frankly about blow job techniques and sex stuff in a way that attracted the attention of the noxious Dave Portnoy at Barstool Sports. After a messy contract dispute that found Franklyn leaving the podcast, Cooper took the reins herself and left the confessional, messy version of herself in the past to become one of the most influential and most-listened-to podcasters, second only to a small thumb of a man to whom we should pay no mind.

At thirty-one, Cooper is on the tail end of the millennial generation and is a de facto elder stateswoman for the five million listeners who tune in weekly. Cooper's influence and audience are both big enough that she can pull big names, but for me, her biggest get was Leah and Rob, both of whom sat down with her after their eliminations. Listening to Cooper, who is not particularly concise, and Leah talk to each other about everything from accidentally eating too many edibles or a man from Leah's past who literally took her brain and "molded the fuck out of it" is a breathless experience. It's hard to keep up, but what stands out is how the two women are expressing themselves. There's a sort of gallows humor in the way Leah speaks; she's a deadpan Calabasas Daria, just slightly less cynical. It is a compelling combination. Cooper brings up an incident at Movie Night, when the Islanders watched some troubling unaired footage that put many of their already-tenuous relationships in jeopardy. Leah found herself at the center of an argument involving Kaylor Martin, a pouty blond who cries with reckless abandon, aspirationally so, like, every two episodes. Leah's recap of what went down is poetry:

"I literally said the balcony, and she's like, [large, dramatic inhale], and I was like, and then Serena was like, 'Don't be dramatic,' and I'm like, 'It was literally giving white woman scared.'

## Megan C. Reynolds

And I said the word 'balcony,' and then she, like, ducked like I was about to, like, hit her with the right hook."

If you read that sentence out loud, there's a rhythm here that's sort of pleasing, each "literally" and "like" jabbing like a fingernail digging into the soft flesh of your arm. Without these words used in these particular ways, the story is staid, boring, and not worth your time. The way Leah tells this to Cooper is vaguely specific, so that if you've watched the show, you know exactly what she's talking about, and if you haven't, you must find out. About forty-five minutes in, Cooper gets down to brass tacks and asks about the aforementioned snake handler, Rob, who Leah was initially paired up with. "Passengers, all aboard, we have now arrived at Rob Island," Leah says. "But literally," Cooper says in response—an electrifying way to use this word that I had not yet heard! Using "literally" as a response in a conversation where you are emphatically agreeing with the other person adds just a soupçon of meaning to your assent. Sure, you could say "Right!" or "Totally!" or "exactly" or "yeah," but "literally" is hyperbolic in a way that's brushing up against your true feelings. Cooper's good at her job, and she knows the material—her agreement is following Leah's lead in the tone of the conversation, and she's also validating Leah's experience. No, it was not literally Rob Island, but in the thick of it, trapped in the bubble of the villa, to Leah, it almost literally was.

For me, the idea of significant change is fine, but in practice, it can fuck itself; I dislike the mess and don't love that the outcome is unknowable. And because of this garden-variety anxiety, saying precisely what I mean in the way I want it to sound is important to me, because I sometimes think that if I get my words exactly right, something unlocks and I will be able to control the outcome. Of course, this isn't true. If someone is, at their very core, an asshole, then that state of being is immovable and you can't change their essence, and so any major or minor conflict with someone who's just kind of a dick will end up leaving you gobsmacked and gaslighting yourself into thinking it was something you said. The truth of the matter is simple: There is no way you can affect the outcome of a situation by saying things differently. What's going to happen is going to happen, it is out of your hands, and the sooner you can believe this to be true, then something that looks and feels like peace awaits.

It is briefly alarming to think about the myriad ways we have to express ourselves, because the vast number of options means that there definitely, *absolutely* is a "right" way to say it, and you gotta kiss a lot of frogs before you find a prince. But options allow, ironically, for precision. We should find joy in this exercise because it allows for expression, nuance, and clarity. Filler words don't gunk up the works; they keep the chains oiled so that the entire machine runs smoothly. And the goal of any conversation is not just communication but also connection, all underscored by the desire to feel seen and heard, two nightmarish but ultimately worthwhile sensations that every person deserves.

Any word that can possibly help achieve that goal is worthy of our attention. And filler words, regardless of how superfluous they may actually *feel*, *are* necessary. Of all the various horrors that we endure daily in this world, from war to famine to stepping in dog shit on the way to the train, your barista saying that your matcha will be ready in, like, five minutes ranks pretty low on the list. To stand in opposition against "like" and its friends is energy better spent doing anything else. As I remind myself far more often than is healthy, death will come for us all one day. Make your time here feel meaningful. Make connections, find new ones. Speak freely and tell people how you feel—and make sure they hear you, whatever it takes. It's, like, the one and only way to live a decent and fulfilling life.

# References

### Introduction: Like, Why?

Beck, Jennifer, Jaymie Bernardo, Theo Chen, Karl Danielsen, and Calista Eaton-Steinberg. 2021. "Yeah, Um . . . So Like, Are Filler Words Considered Feminine?" *Languaged Life: Studies in Language and Society*, January 18. https://languagedlife.humspace.ucla.edu/sociolinguistics/yeah-um-so-like-are-filler-words-considered-feminine/.

D'Arcy, Alexandra. 2017. *Discourse-Pragmatic Variation in Context: Eight Hundred Years of LIKE*. John Benjamins Publishing Company.

Gissen, Lillian. 2023. "Are YOU Suffering from the Influencer Inflection? Furious Debate Breaks Out Over 'Irritating' Voice Used by Online Stars." *Daily Mail*, November 22. https://www.dailymail.co.uk/femail/article-12776693/Influencer-inflection-online-stars-tone-voice.html.

Montell, Amanda. 2019. *Wordslut: A Feminist Guide to Taking Back the English Language*. Harper Wave.

Pritchard, Emma [@eemmamacdonald]. 2022. "3 min GRWM | PRODUCTS I USED LINKED IN MY BIO UNDER MAKEUP FAVS #sephorasale." TikTok, November 2. https://www.tiktok.com/@eemmamacdonald/video/7161443824059895082.

Sapir, Edward. 1921. *Language: An Introduction to the Study of Speech*. Harcourt, Brace and Company.

# References

Schwarz, Hunter. 2017. "Why This Millennial Democrat's Concession Speech Sounds Like He's Doing an Obama Impression." CNN, June 21. www.cnn.com/2017/06/21/politics/ossoff-concession-obama-cadence/index.html.

Stamper, Kory. 2017. *Word by Word: The Secret Life of Dictionaries*. Pantheon Books.

Svitek, Patrick. 2022. "Beto O'Rourke Swears at Greg Abbott Supporter Who Heckled Him Over Uvalde Shooting." *The Texas Tribune*, August 11. www.texastribune.org/2022/08/11/beto-orourke-greg-abbott-motherfucker-heckler/.

Wallace, K. 2016. "Why You Should Stop Saying 'Like' So Much." CNN, August 16. https://www.cnn.com/2016/08/16/health/parent-acts-saying-like-verbal-bad-habits/index.html.

## Chapter 1: Like, What?

D'Arcy, Alexandra. 2017. *Discourse-Pragmatic Variation in Context: Eight Hundred Years of LIKE*. John Benjamins Publishing Company.

Grant, Adam. 2023. "Women Know Exactly What They're Doing When They Use 'Weak Language.'" *New York Times*, July 31. www.nytimes.com/2023/07/31/opinion/women-language-work.html.

Lakoff, Robin. 1973. "Language and Woman's Place." *Language in Society* 2 (1): 45–80.

Lockwood, Charles. 2016. "Clark Gable and Carole Lombard's House in California." *Architectural Digest*, August 30. www.architecturaldigest.com/story/clark-gable-carole-lombard-ranch-home-california.

Los Angeles County Library. n.d. "San Fernando Local History." Accessed October 24, 2024. https://lacountylibrary.org/sanfernando-local-history/.

McFadden, Robert D. 2019. "John Simon, Wide-Ranging Critic with a Cutting Pen, Dies at 94." *New York Times*, November 25. www.nytimes.com/2019/11/25/arts/john-simon-dead.html.

Pond, Mimi. 1982. *The Valley Girl's Guide to Life*. Dell Publishing Company.

Skinner, David. 2009. "Ain't That the Truth." *Humanities* 30 (4). www.neh.gov/humanities/2009/julyaugust/feature/ain%E2%80%99t-the-truth.

Tolentino, Jia. 2024. "What Tweens Get from Sephora and What They Get

# References

from Us." *New Yorker*, August 10. www.newyorker.com/culture/the-weekend-essay/what-tweens-get-from-sephora-and-what-they-get-from-us.

Universal Music Group. 2022. "Frank Zappa's Satirical, Acid-Tongued 'Valley Girl' Like, Totally Turns 40; Celebrated with First-Ever Video Out Today." Grateful Web, September 16. www.gratefulweb.com/articles/frank-zappas-satirical-acid-tongued-valley-girl-totally-turns-40-celebrated-first-ever.

Waldek, Stefanie. 2022. "Rare Vintage Photos of Lucille Ball's Life at Her Many Homes." *House Beautiful*, January 18. www.housebeautiful.com/design-inspiration/celebrity-homes/g38775964/lucille-ball-home-photos/.

## Interlude: The Grammar Wars

O'Conner, Patricia T., and Stewart Kellerman. 2009. *Origins of the Specious: Myths and Misconceptions of the English Language.* Random House.

University of California, San Francisco. n.d. "U.S. Culture." Accessed October 24, 2024. https://isso.ucsf.edu/us-culture.

## Chapter 2: And *Then* I Was Like . . .

Brown, Brené. 2012. *The Power of Vulnerability: Teachings on Authenticity, Connection, and Courage.* Sounds True.

Jacobs, A. J. 2007. "I Think You're Fat." *Esquire*, July 24. www.esquire.com/news-politics/a26792/honesty0707/.

Radical Candor. n.d. "Video Tip: What Is Radical Candor? Learn the Basic Principles in 6 Minutes." Accessed October 24, 2024. www.radicalcandor.com/blog/what-is-radical-candor/.

Radical Honesty Institute. n.d. "Radical Honesty." Accessed October 24, 2024. www.radicalhonesty.com.

## Chapter 3: Well, Like, I Just, I'm Not, Like, Sure . . .

ABC News. 2008. "Full Transcript of the Gibson Interviews Sarah Palin." November 23. abcnews.go.com/Politics/Vote2008/full-transcript-gibson-interviews-sarah-palin/story?id=9159105.

Cohen, Steven D. 2012. "Tips on Public Speaking: Eliminating the Dreaded

# References

'Um.'" Harvard Extension School, extension.harvard.edu/blog/tips-on-public-speaking-eliminating-the-dreaded-um/.

Demopoulos, Alaina. 2024. "'kamala IS brat': Harris Campaign Goes Lime-Green to Embrace the Meme of the Summer." *The Guardian*, July 23. www.theguardian.com/us-news/article/2024/jul/23/kamala-harris-charli-xcx-brat.

Dupré, Maggie Harrison. 2023. "Sports Illustrated Published Articles by Fake, AI-Generated Writers." Futurism, November 27. www.futurism.com/sports-illustrated-ai-generated-writers.

Hess, Amanda. 2015. "Yas We Can: The Curious Social Media Strategy of Hillary Clinton's Campaign." *Slate*, December 15. www.slate.com/technology/2015/12/hillary-clinton-speaks-like-a-millennial-on-social-media.html.

Macmanus, Annie, and Nick Grimshaw, hosts. 2024. *Sidetracked with Annie and Nick*. "Sidetracked with Charli XCX." BBC Sounds, June 6. Podcast, 27 min., 41 sec. www.bbc.co.uk/sounds/play/p0j2f1ql.

Nowell, Cecilia. 2024. "How Tim Walz Went from NRA Favorite to 'Straight Fs' on Gun Rights." *The Guardian*, August 9. www.theguardian.com/us-news/article/2024/aug/09/tim-walz-gun-control-stance.

Pellish, Aaron, Andrew Kaczynski, and Em Steck. 2024. "Walz Says He 'Misspoke' After Unearthed Newspaper Reports Undercut Claim He Was in Hong Kong During Tiananmen Square Protests." CNN, October 1. www.cnn.com/2024/10/01/politics/tim-walz-china-tiananmen-square/index.html.

Siegel, Muffy E. A. 2002. "*Like*: The Discourse Particle and Semantics." *Journal of Semantics* 19 (1): 35–71. https://doi.org/10.1093/jos/19.1.35.

Writers Guild of America West. 2024. "Know Your Rights: Artificial Intelligence." Last modified September 18. www.wga.org/contracts/know-your-rights/artificial-intelligence.

Yurcaba, Jo. 2024. "Some LGBTQ People React to Kamala Harris' Run with Viral Memes, Campy T-shirts." NBC News, July 22. https://www.nbcnews.com/nbc-out/out-politics-and-policy/kamala-harris-queer-fans-viral-memes-rcna163088.

## Interlude: But What About Texting?

Ehrenreich, Samuel E., Kurt J. Beron, Kaitlyn Burnell, Diana J. Meter, and Marion K. Underwood. 2019. "How Adolescents Use Text Messaging

# References

Through Their High School Years." *Journal of Research on Adolescence* 30 (2): 521–540. https://doi.org/10.1111/jora.12541.

Mulqueen, Maggie. 2019. "Texting Really Is Ruining Personal Relationships." NBC News, December 7. www.nbcnews.com/think/opinion/texting-really-ruining-personal-relationships-ncna1097461.

Perlman, Merrill. 2018. "*Merriam-Webster* and *OED* Add New Words: Lorem ipsum, TL;DR, and More." *Columbia Journalism Review*, September 24. www.cjr.org/language_corner/lorem-ipsum-tldr.php.

## Interlude: Brass Tacks (Dictionaries)

Koenig, John. 2021. *The Dictionary of Obscure Sorrows*. Simon & Schuster.

Stamper, Kory. 2017. *Word by Word: The Secret Life of Dictionaries*. Pantheon Books.

## Chapter 4: I Have, Like, One Zillion Things to Do

Dreyer, Benjamin. 2019. *Dreyer's English: An Utterly Correct Guide to Clarity and Style*. Random House.

Fuller, Janet M. 2003. "Use of the Discourse Marker *Like* in Interviews." *Journal of Sociolinguistics* 7 (3): 365–377. https://doi.org/10.1111/1467-9481.00229.

Sun, Wei. 2013. "The Importance of Discourse Markers in English Learning and Teaching." *Theory and Practice in Language Studies* 3 (11): 2136–2140. https://doi.org/10.4304/tpls.3.11.2136-2140.

## Interlude: Why Is It Women?

Eckert, Penelope. 1989. *Jocks and Burnouts: Social Categories and Identity in the High School*. Teachers College Press.

Eckert, Penelope. 2003. "Language and Adolescent Peer Groups." *Journal of Language and Social Psychology* 22 (1): 112–118. https://doi.org/10.1177/0261927X02250063.

Labov, William. 1990. "The Intersection of Sex and Social Class in the Course of Linguistic Change." *Language Variation and Change* 2 (2): 205–254. https://doi.org/10.1017/S0954394500000338.

# References

Tagliamonte, Sali A., and Alexandra D'Arcy. 2009. "Peaks Beyond Phonology: Adolescence, Incrementation, and Language Change." *Language* 85 (1): 58–108. https://dx.doi.org/10.1353/lan.0.0084.

## Chapter 5: Like, It's Sexist?

Ehrlich, Richard S. 2013. "The Man Who Founded a Religion Based on 'The Big Lebowski.'" CNN Travel, March 20. https://web.archive.org/web/20130324030503/http://travel.cnn.com/bangkok/life/doctrine-chiang-mais-church-latter-day-dude-explained-206793/.

Eutsey, Dwayne. n.d. "The Take It Easy Manifesto." Accessed October 24, 2024. http://dudeism.com/takeiteasymanifesto/.

Felson Duchan, Judith. 2001. "The Elocution Movement." University at Buffalo. https://www.acsu.buffalo.edu/~duchan/new_history/hist19c/elocution.html.

Glass, Lillian. 1982. *How to Deprogram Your Valley Girl*. Workman Publishing.

Hill, Richard A. 1994. "You've Come a Long Way, Dude: A History." *American Speech* 69 (3): 321–327. https://doi.org/10.2307/455525.

Kiesling, Scott F. 2004. "Dude." *American Speech* 79 (3): 281–305. https://doi.org/10.1215/00031283-79-3-281.

Mele, Christopher. 2017. "So, Um, How Do You, Like, Stop Using Filler Words?" *New York Times*, February 24. www.nytimes.com/2017/02/24/us/verbal-ticks-like-um.html.

Wolf, Naomi. 2015. "Young Women, Give Up the Vocal Fry and Reclaim Your Strong Female Voice." *The Guardian*, July 24. www.theguardian.com/commentisfree/2015/jul/24/vocal-fry-strong-female-voice.

## Interlude: Girls on Film

Crowther, Bosley. 1953. "The Screen in Review: 'Gentlemen Prefer Blondes' at Roxy, with Marilyn Monroe and Jane Russell." *New York Times*, July 16. www.nytimes.com/1953/07/16/archives/the-screen-in-review-gentlemen-prefer-blondes-at-roxy-with-marilyn.html.

Loftus, Jamie, and Caitlin Durante, hosts. 2018. *The Bechdel Cast*. "Gentlemen Prefer Blondes with Karina Longworth." iHeart Podcasts, November 15.

Podcast, 60 min., 38 sec. https://www.iheart.com/podcast/105-the-bechdel-cast-30089535/episode/gentlemen-prefer-blondes-with-karina-longworth-30155521.

## Interlude: How Do People Learn English?

Ives, Mike. 2021. "How 'Friends' Helps People Around the World Learn English." *New York Times*, May 29. www.nytimes.com/2021/05/29/arts/television/friends-reunion-english.html.

## Interlude: Nǐ Shuō Shénme?!

Change.org. n.d. "Re-instate USC Marshall Professor Greg Patton." Accessed October 24, 2024. www.change.org/p/university-of-southern-california-re-instate-usc-marshall-professor-greg-patton?source_location=topic_page.

Ethier, Marc. 2020. "USC Marshall Prof Suspended After Using a Chinese Term That Sounds Similar to the N-Word." Poets & Quants, September 4. https://poetsandquants.com/2020/09/04/usc-marshall-prof-suspended-after-using-a-chinese-term-that-is-similar-to-the-n-word/2/.

Flaherty, Colleen. 2020. "Failure to Communicate: Professor Suspended for Saying Chinese Word That Sounds Like English Slur." Inside Higher Ed, September 7. https://www.insidehighered.com/news/2020/09/08/professor-suspended-saying-chinese-word-sounds-english-slur.

Friedersdorf, Conor. 2021. "The Fight Against Words That Sound Like, But Are Not, Slurs." *The Atlantic*, September 21. https://www.theatlantic.com/ideas/archive/2020/09/fight-against-words-sound-like-are-not-slurs/616404/.

Mandarin HQ. n.d. "Speak Like a Local: Why & How Native Speakers Use Filler Words in Chinese." Accessed October 24, 2024. www.mandarinhq.com/2024/04/chinese-filler-words/.

Wang, Aiqing. 2021. "Inter-lingual Homophony: Neige as a Demonstrative/Filler in Mandarin Chinese." *Studia Orientalia Electronica* 9 (1): 138–153. https://doi.org/10.23993/store.102506.

Yeung, Jessie. 2020. "USC Professor Under Fire After Using Chinese Expression Students Allege Sounds Like English Slur." CNN, September 10. www.cnn.com/2020/09/10/us/usc-chinese-professor-racism-intl-hnk-scli/index.html.

# References

Yoyo Chinese. n.d. "Um and Uh in Chinese: 8 Essential Filler Words." Accessed October 24, 2024. https://yoyochinese.com/blog/learn-mandarin-chinese-filler-words-um-and-uh-in-chinese.

Zeigler, Cyd. 2012. "ESPN Uses Racial Epithet in Headline of Jeremy Lin Story." Outsports, February 17. www.outsports.com/2012/2/17/4052616/espn-uses-racial-epithet-in-headline-of-jeremy-lin-story.

## Chapter 6: That's, Like, Not Very Professional

Bay, Samara. 2023. *Permission to Speak: How to Change What Power Sounds Like, Starting with You.* Crown.

United States Department of Labor. 2021. "Skills to Pay the Bills: Mastering Soft Skills for Workplace Success." www.dol.gov/sites/dolgov/files/ODEP/IntroMasteringSoftSkillsforWorkplaceSuccess.pdf.

Van Zuylen-Wood, Simon. 2012. "Terry Gross: The Queen of 'Like.'" *Philadelphia*, December 21. www.phillymag.com/news/2012/12/21/npr-terry-gross-queen-like/.

## Chapter 7: Like . . . !

Dreyer, Benjamin. 2019. *Dreyer's English: An Utterly Correct Guide to Clarity and Style.* Random House.

Granovetter, Mark S. 1973. "The Strength of Weak Ties." *American Journal of Sociology* 78 (6): 1360–1380. http://www.jstor.org/stable/2776392.

Haile, Heven. 2023. "*Like..? EP.*" *Pitchfork*, January 23. www.pitchfork.com/reviews/albums/ice-spice-like-ep/.

Ihaza, Jeff. 2022. "How Ice Spice Added a Touch of Zest to New York's Drill Scene." *Rolling Stone*, October 14. www.rollingstone.com/music/music-features/ice-spice-interview-munch-1234608104/.

McCulloch, Gretchen. 2019. *Because Internet: Understanding the New Rules of Language.* Riverhead Books.

Rose, Jordan. 2022. "A Guide to Modern New York Drill Slang." Complex, October 28. www.complex.com/music/a/j-rose/new-york-drill-slang-defined.

# References

Urban Dictionary. n.d. "Munch." Accessed October 24, 2024. www.urban dictionary.com/define.php?term=Munch.

## Conclusion: Like, What's Next?

Cooper, Alex, host. 2024. *Call Her Daddy*. "Leah's Love Island Tell All." Spotify, July 26. https://open.spotify.com/episode/4JGMvHzWUMlaO3vsV BaTzE.

Cronkite, Walter. 2011. "Walter Cronkite on His First and Only Commercial for Winston Cigarettes - EMMYTVLEGENDS.ORG." Interview. Posted June 30, by FoundationINTERVIEWS. YouTube, 3:16. www.youtube.com /watch?v=HrdfEsVVx9U.

Dickson, EJ. 2023. "Alex Cooper Went from Raunchy Podcaster to Gen-Z's Barbara Walters." *Rolling Stone*, September 19. www.rollingstone.com /culture/culture-features/alex-cooper-call-her-daddy-podcast-empire -1234827373/.

Hartston, William. 1998. "Why to Boldly Split Your Infinitives Is Now Acceptable Oxford English." *Independent*, August 12. www.independent.co .uk/news/why-to-boldly-split-your-infinitives-is-now-acceptable-oxford -english-1171281.html.

Max Planck Institute for Human Cognitive and Brain Sciences. 2024. "Learning a Second Language Is Transforming the Brain." Last modified January 8. www.cbs.mpg.de/2206561/20230108.

University of Nevada, Reno. n.d. "British and American English." Accessed October 24, 2024. www.unr.edu/writing-speaking-center/writing-speaking -resources/british-american-english.

Woodward English. 2024. "Pronunciation of Final -S." Last modified September 29. www.grammar.cl/english/pronunciation-final-s.htm.

Zarinsky, Natasha. 2014. "What the Hell Is Up with 'Bae'?" *Esquire*, July 25. www.esquire.com/lifestyle/news/a29423/where-did-bae-come-from/.

## Acknowledgments

Writing a book is hard and lonely until it very much is not—and that would be at the end of the thing when all is said and done.

Thanking people without sounding glib is not my forte, but please know that I am grateful for everyone listed in these pages. Thank you to my agent, David Paterson, who endured many panicked emails with grace and patience. At HarperCollins, my editor, Rakesh Satyal, saved me from potential idiocy, and, without him, this book would truly not exist. Thank you to Ryan Amato, who answered every question and did so with kindness; Kaitlyn San Miguel's copyedits are half the reason this thing is worth reading in the first place.

Thank you to all the experts, friends, and family who lent their voice and knowledge, filling in the blanks that were much, much needed: Andy Rinaldi and Steve Campagna, for their insights into what goes on behind the boards of your favorite podcast; and Bobby Finger and Lindsey Weber, the faces of your favorite artist's favorite podcast, *Who? Weekly*, for their insights about what happens on the other side. The writings of Alexandra D'Arcy

## Acknowledgments

and Muffy E. A. Siegel were invaluable, and they both graciously lent their time to a writer who is decidedly not a linguist. Isabella Sarmiento Gomez, Samara Bey, Mimi Pond, Winnie Liao, and my mom, Sui-fen Liao, all generously shared their time and experiences with me, and, without them, this book would not be what it is now.

Many friends and loved ones provided support throughout this process, and while the thought of forgetting someone is the demon that haunts my nightmares, I'm going to try not to. In no particular order: to Julianne Escobedo Shepherd, Joanna Rothkopf, Katie McDonough, Clover Hope, Ellie Shechet, Clio Chang, Hazel Cills, Anne Branigin, Alex Balk, Mike Dang, Kelly Conaboy, Julia Sheng, Esther Wang, Molly Osberg, Anna Merlan, Kate Dries, Emma Carmichael, Jia Tolentino, Stassa Edwards, Kelly Faircloth, Jack Balderrama Morley and the entire staff of *Dwell*, my therapist Thomas Wells, Sam Woolley, Gabi Sifre, Emily Alford, Erica Hirsch, Wendy Mainardi, Greg Hastings, Stephen Caputo, and Sonia Replansky—thank you all for reading a chapter or talking me through a moment of panic or generally being there for me even despite my resistance.

Thanks to my family Sui-fen Liao and Ross Travis, David Reynolds and Diana Devlin, for your care, support, and love. To my precious and darling sisters, Jenny, Tessa, and Shaina, thank you (I guess!) for the group chat that I will never delete from my phone. Thanks to Daisy (a cat), who graciously, despite her old age, stayed alive throughout this process. For everyone mentioned here, and even those I may have forgotten, I refuse to say it out loud, so I'll say it in print instead. I love you all very much.

**About the Author**

Megan C. Reynolds is an editor at *Dwell* magazine and previously worked at *Jezebel* and *The Billfold*. She's written for *BuzzFeed*, *The New York Times*, *Elle*, *Gawker*, *Bustle*, *Vulture*, and other outlets. Reynolds was also the cohost of the short-lived celebrity-gossip-focused podcast *Dirtcast*. She lives in New York City.